A Heritage of Faith

A Heritage of Faith

Talks Selected from the BYU Women's Conferences

Edited by Mary E. Stovall and Carol Cornwall Madsen

Camilla Eyring Kimball • Carol Cornwall Madsen

Patricia Terry Holland • Harriet Horne Arrington

Dallin H. Oaks • Leonard J. Arrington

Carolyn J. Rasmus • Betty Ventura

Francine R. Bennion • Val D. MacMurray

Deanne Francis • John P. Hawkins

Stephen J. Bahr • Karen Lynn Davidson

Anne L. Horton • Louise Plummer

Deseret Book Company
Salt Lake City, Utah

First printing March 1988

Library of Congress Cataloging-in-Publication Data

A Heritage of faith : talks selected from the BYU women's conferences
    / edited by Mary E. Stovall and Carol Cornwall Madsen.
        p.   cm.

Includes bibliographies and index.
1. Women—Religious life.   2. Spiritual life—Mormon authors.
3. Women in the Mormon Church.   I. Stovall, Mary Elizabeth, 1951-
II. Madsen, Carol Cornwall, 1930-   III. Brigham Young
University.
BX8641.H47   1988   289.3'32'088042—dc19   87-36512
ISBN 0-87579-130-1   CIP

Contents

Contents

"And as all have not faith, seek ye diligently and teach one another words of wisdom." (D&C 88:118.) With the hope that the words in this volume will edify, uplift, and instruct those who read them, we have compiled carefully selected presentations from the 1985, 1986, and 1987 Brigham Young University Women's Conferences. Included are talks that we believe perceptively and affirmatively address vital issues in the lives of all thoughtful Latter-day Saints. The authors of the essays examine the issues honestly and openly, neither afraid of hard questions nor satisfied with easy answers. We hope readers of this volume will find new understanding and angles of vision and, most of all, peace, hope, and comfort in confronting the daily struggles and joys of life.

The first section, "Developing Spirituality," focuses explicitly on our identity as women of faith and women of God. Camilla Eyring Kimball examines the totality of commitment required to be a woman of faith and gently and humorously illustrates the process of becoming such through examples from her own life. Patricia Terry Holland cautions us to love each other and avoid judgments despite apparent differences in talents, experience, and opportunity. In a scriptural examination of spiritual gifts, Elder Dallin H. Oaks challenges us to seek for those gifts we lack to strengthen us and our ability to serve. The final essay of the section, by Carolyn J. Rasmus, reflects on her conversion to the gospel and the legacy she will leave future generations.

"Coping with Hard Realities," the second section, raises questions about the nature of pain and suffering and the reasons for them and offers strategies for understanding and dealing with them. In the keynote essay to the section, Francine R. Bennion uses her vast knowledge of the scriptures to explore explanations for suffering and how we can come to terms with it. Deanne Francis discusses the stages of grief and, with great compassion, relates experiences that define what is helpful and what is hurtful to those in pain. Stephen J. Bahr analyzes another type of stress, the economic dislocation that accompanies divorce, and surveys the effects on women of changes in divorce laws. In the final essay of this section, Anne L. Horton examines the effects of personal violence and challenges us to eliminate any vestiges of violence from our own lives and to understand and assist those who suffer abuse.

The third section, "Inspiration from the Past," asks us to consider how women of the past influence women of today through the continuing relevance of their experience and example. Carol Cornwall Madsen examines the development of personal faith and commitment by Elizabeth Ann Whitney and places her experiences and those of her contemporary Mormon sisters into the broader context of women's religious experiences in nineteenth-century America. Harriet Horne Arrington and Leonard J. Arrington then focus on the life-long commitment to community service demonstrated by Alice Merrill Horne, the "first lady of Utah arts," who labored tirelessly for the cultural enrichment and welfare of Utah.

The essays in section four, "Women in an International Church," are appeals to increase our awareness of the culturally diverse lives and values of members of the Church beyond the boundaries of the United States. Betty Ventura graphically illustrates difficulties in transferring the gospel message across cultures but also notes lessons American Mormons can learn from those of other cultural traditions. Using the life of his daughter Heidi as a foil, Val D. MacMurray discusses typical experiences and expectations of young women in third-world countries and challenges us to become involved in broadening the disadvantaged lives they live. In the concluding essay of this section, John P. Hawkins reflects on insights obtained from his research in Guatemala: that in transmitting the gospel around the world, we must express truth in the specific cultural idiom of each nation rather than requiring worldwide conformity to American culture, whose practices may be misunderstood by those we wish to interest in the gospel.

Preface

The final section, "Individuality and Community," raises questions about identity, diversity, and mutual support in the quest for Christlike lives. Karen Lynn Davidson considers the positive and negative effects of peer pressure, and Louise Plummer offers a humorous look at the need for individuality.

This volume is one in a series of collected talks on a variety of topics from the BYU Women's Conferences. We hope that the publication of these addresses will further the continuing quest for both greater understanding of life and increased religious conviction.

Mary E. Stovall and
Carol Cornwall Madsen

SEEKING SPIRITUALITY

If "the glory of God is intelligence, or in other words light and truth" (D&C 93:36), then it is our responsibility to gather truth of all sorts, not just truths of theology, but of everything.

— CAMILLA EYRING KIMBALL

Women of Faith

CAMILLA EYRING KIMBALL

When I was young I anticipated birthdays, seeing them as a mark of advancement and as opening the door to new opportunities. Then in middle age I dreaded birthdays, because they represented the closing of some doors and the approach of debilitating old age. But as I got older still—to the "My, you're looking wonderful!" stage—I started to look forward to birthdays again. There is even a temptation to exaggerate a little, because each birthday shows something of an achievement—showing that I have managed to hang on through one more cycle of the seasons. I celebrated my ninetieth birthday just a few months ago. That was quite a surprise to me, because for a whole year I had been saying I was already ninety.

Except for a little pride in surviving, I can say from experience that old age is not a status to envy, because there's not much future in it. Unfortunately, old age is a time of aches and pains, and a time of unwanted dependency on others after a lifetime of being self-sufficient. It is a time of gradually slowing down. And there is a frustrating sense that there are a thousand

Camilla Eyring Kimball, beloved former "first lady" of the Church, was a strong advocate of education. She held a teaching certificate from Brigham Young University and was awarded an honorary doctor of humane letters degree by the University of Utah. In recognition of her many years of community and Church service and for her support of lifelong learning, BYU established an endowed chair, the Camilla Eyring Kimball Chair of Home and Family Life, in her honor. Sister Kimball served in numerous ward and stake callings in the women's organizations, including more than sixty years as a visiting teacher. She was an avid gardener and then turned to oil painting in her tenth decade.

Sister Kimball delivered this keynote address at the 1985 BYU Women's Conference.

things still undone and not enough time remaining. But on the other hand, old age does allow one time for reflecting with some satisfaction on the joys and accomplishments of a lifetime.

There are some advantages to old age, though. Now that my memory has faded a bit, I find I can enjoy reading a book the second time. I enjoyed rereading the biography of my husband and, as I read along, I kept wondering how it would all turn out!

But more seriously, there is a measure of satisfaction that as we get older we keep coming closer and closer to "enduring to the end" by being faithful to the important values in life.

What are those values which are so important to hold onto until the very end? Christ told us what is most fundamental:

"Behold, a certain lawyer stood up, and tempted him, saying, Master, what shall I do to inherit eternal life?

"He said unto him, What is written in the law? how readest thou?

"And he answering said, Thou shalt love the Lord thy God with all thy heart, and with all thy soul, and with all thy strength, and with all thy mind; and thy neighbor as thyself.

"And he said unto him, Thou has answered right: this do, and thou shalt live." (Luke 10:25–28.)

A woman of faith, then, is one whose heart and soul, mind and strength are committed to the pursuit of true values. First, in her heart and soul, a faithful woman acknowledges God's role in all things. Then, with her mind she seeks to understand the divine plan for this world. And finally, with the strength of her hands, she undertakes to carry out the fundamental tasks of mankind, which are to keep God's commandments and give unselfish service to His children.

First, faith. "Without faith it is impossible to please [God]: for he that cometh to God must believe that he is, and that he is a rewarder of them that diligently seek him." (Hebrews 11:6.)

I am not able to get around as much as I once did, and as a result I have looked at more television than I ever did in my younger years. In watching television I like best of all the programs that tell me about nature. Television is my substitute for travel. Through the marvel of the magic box I can be

4

transported in an instant anywhere. I can travel through a telescope to outer space or through a microscope to the recesses of the human brain.

Whether it is bees or polar bears, whales or forests, I am fascinated by the fantastic variety and intricate interdependency of the various forms of life. I marvel at God's creation in its infinite complexity. I am much too unlettered to begin understanding the grand design of God, but like one who stands before a great tapestry, I can drink in its beauty and stand admiring its intricacy without knowing exactly how the artist achieved the effect. I know God's hand is in nature. I do not know just *how* God created the world, but I am persuaded that He *did* it, and I stand in awe and wonder at the majesty of His creation. My heart is full of gratitude toward a loving Father.

Second, when we have obtained faith in the Great Creator, we are inclined to want to know what it is that would please God. He has said that He wants us to love Him with all our mind.

I believe that to love God with our *mind* means to pursue understanding of His world. We are to develop the talents God has given us. There are many kinds of talents, many gifts—faith and healing, music and art, leadership and followership, and intellect, the capacity for learning. Though they are all valuable gifts, it is the last that I would emphasize here partly because of the university setting and partly because of my personal inclinations. Though we may have *other* gifts as well, all of us gathered here share the marvelous ability to acquire knowledge. We are taught that we should "seek learning, even by study and also by faith." (D&C 88:118.)

I love to study; I love to learn. At one time I learned for the sheer pleasure of learning. Now I do it more for the purpose of understanding God's great creation and my role in it. As a result, I don't read much fiction any more. In the past few months I have read a book of essays that gave me new insights into gospel principles. I finished the Book of Mormon again, which ends on a stirring challenge to be "perfect in Christ." (Moroni 10:33.) *A Marvelous Work and a Wonder*, by LeGrand Richards, got me thinking about the urgent preparations we need to make against the troubles of the last days. And I have read several biographies. When I read biographies, I am looking to see how God's plan works itself out in the lives of men and women. And as I read the scriptures, I stand amazed at how I can fall so far short of living all the commandments and yet know that God loves me anyway.

If "the glory of God is intelligence, or in other words light and truth" (D&C 93:36), then it is our responsibility to gather truth of all sorts, not just truths of theology, but of everything. So long as we do not become vain in our learning, it is all to the good.

There are various ways of learning—reading, discussing, and experiencing. I wish I could be in the classroom again. Books are good, but there is something special about the interchange of ideas in the classroom. I look forward each week to Sunday School and Relief Society for the stimulation I get there. And I have found that participation in community affairs gives me new and important insights.

I have always wanted desperately to increase my education. In 1912, at age seventeen, I came to Provo as a refugee from the Mexican Revolution, to finish high school and earn a teaching certificate. One day I received a telegram from my father asking why I had not written a letter. The reason was that I did not have two cents for a stamp. But I could not give up school. Being a student and becoming a teacher were both my pleasure and my need.

Many of the people who came to BYU in those days were here at considerable sacrifice. Education was hard to come by and recognized as a precious commodity. But that is still true. Many students here today have chosen a hard road, but they are coming into possession of a fund of knowledge beyond the dreams of most people in the world. It carries with it great power for good or ill.

As a young teacher, I planned to alternate working and going to school until I had completed a graduate degree in dietetics. As it turned out, I met Spencer Kimball and married instead. That kept me from finishing my specific educational goal, but it did not stop me from being curious, nor did it stop my learning, because regular schooling is just one of the ways of becoming educated.

Reading books has opened a thousand doors for me. I worked through the Women's Club in Arizona to help establish a public library in the little farming town where we lived in order to open those same doors for others. We also benefited from having a college nearby, which provided some community education classes. And I was always active in Church teaching. As a Japanese proverb says, "To teach is to learn." I enjoyed the challenge to understanding that is a prerequisite to effective teaching.

I always did my best to encourage my brothers and sisters and my children to take advantage of educational opportunities. If there was a price to be paid, in money or effort, I considered it well worth the price.

I have found from my own experience in taking courses at the institute of religion and at the University of Utah after we moved to Salt Lake City that there is joy in learning, that it helps keep us young in spirit, and that, whatever the subject — religion or Spanish or typing or literature — it enlarges our capacity for service.

Learning is not just for one set of people or for one time of life. It is a basic activity for all mankind. We are on earth to learn — first of all the principles of salvation, and then the secrets of the world, to subdue it and make it fruitful, and to delight the mind. The Lord fosters beauty, and there is beauty in all knowledge, not just in music and painting, but in biology and geology and mathematics, too.

I know well the limits of my understanding. I make no pretension to great knowledge in any field, but I offer no apology. In comparison to our Heavenly Father, even the most learned person knows nothing. The process of education, aside from its pleasure, disciplines the mind and makes it our useful servant.

There is some risk in education, of course. It can in a sense become our master rather than our servant. If I may paraphrase another scripture: we have learned by experience that it is the nature and disposition of almost all men, as soon as they get a little *knowledge*, as they suppose, to begin to lord it over others. Learning is one of the great sources of pride. Nephi cried out, "O the wise, and the *learned*, and the rich, that are puffed up in the pride of their hearts ... wo be unto them, saith the Lord God Almighty, for they shall be thrust down to hell!" (2 Nephi 28:15; italics added.) And he wrote also:

"O that cunning plan of the evil one! O the vainness, and the frailties, and the foolishness of men! When they are learned they think they are wise, and they hearken not unto the counsel of God, for they set it aside, supposing they know of themselves, wherefore, their wisdom is foolishness and it profiteth them not. And they shall perish.

"But to be learned is good *if* they hearken unto the counsels of God." (2 Nephi 9:28–29; italics added.)

Nephi is not criticizing learning. On the contrary, he exalts learning as a good thing. He points out that learning has its risks. But on the other hand, ignorance has its risks, too—just a different set.

Though at the time I did not often think of my learning as a religious activity, it clearly was, in the sense that I came to value the inherent goodness in people, to appreciate the world around me, to see the fruits of unselfish cooperation, to increase my sense of self-worth, and to feel I had a capacity to be of service to others.

The third thing a woman of faith will do is to give service to others. Once we have faith in God and have developed the talents and gifts God has given us, and then ask what to do with those abilities, we are told, "Seek ye earnestly the best gifts, always remembering for what they are given ... All these gifts come from God, for the benefit of the children of God." (D&C 46:8, 26.)

Recent First Presidency messages in the *Ensign* have reminded me of my responsibility to strengthen others by my expression of love and confidence and have reminded me of my responsibility to help bring about Zion. Zion will come about only through sacrifice and consecration of our best efforts. If we bring our best gifts, cultivated and polished by faithful effort, together we can build a society where harmony prevails because we have put aside selfishness. I hope that over the years I may have grown a bit less selfish. At least I have tried. And I am reminded to keep on trying by the words of the prophets.

If we examine others' lives, we learn how they have coped with problems and we can take courage in our own difficulties. Whether it is in some great way or in a seemingly insignificant way, each can make a contribution to the whole community.

But we do not know in advance just what part we may be called on to play. Esther was queen of Persia. Her husband, the king, did not know she was a Jew. And when a decree had gone out that all the Jews should be killed, her uncle, Mordecai, appealed to her to step forward and plead with the king for her people. She pointed out to Mordecai that to do so would endanger her own life. He replied, "Who knoweth whether thou art come to the kingdom for such a time as this?" (Esther 4:14.) The question for us is what part we have to play in the great cause. Every bit player is important to the outcome. Let us be ready for our stage entrance.

When I recently reread my husband's life story, I had fun reliving some of the great experiences we have had, and laughing at our foibles, but I also relived the sorrows. I asked myself how that man ever kept on, through all he suffered, until I was reminded that what has motivated him all these years is a fierce loyalty to the Lord and to whatever calling the Lord has given him. He has done *his* best to bring about Zion. Perhaps he was come for such a time as this.

I would like to express my gratitude for the love and support I have received from my husband. Today is his ninetieth birthday [March 28, 1985]. He has served a long and honorable probation. Many people can say by faith that he is a great and good man. I say on the basis of the longest and closest personal experience that there is no finer person in the world. He is the soul of kindness and the embodiment of commitment to do right. He comes wonderfully close to perfection in my opinion.

It is the greatest sorrow of his life, and therefore the greatest sorrow of mine, that he cannot be out among the Saints testifying of Christ and teaching the right path. There is an aching frustration after a long and active life at being so limited in what he can do. He said the other day, with a spark of the old sense of humor, "Resurrection will feel so good after all this."

With all our heart, with all our soul, with all our mind, with all our strength we will love and serve the Lord.

Women of faith will know that the Lord lives and will follow that knowledge, whatever the cost. My great-grandmother Catherine Smith, an English servant girl, was baptized to express her faith in Christ, knowing full well that it might mean the loss of her employment.

Women of faith will learn so that they might be of service. Ellis Shipp went to school to become a doctor, to help meet the needs of her community. In turn, other women cared for her children, so that she could improve her talents.

Women of faith will serve in many ways. While her husband was serving a mission, Caroline Romney Eyring took in boarders, rented her own bed, and slept on the floor rather than let her husband know her financial troubles. And she kept the secret from him that their baby, born after he left, was deaf.

The great women of the scriptures and of our own day give us innumerable examples of spiritual commitment, of the development of talents, and of willing service in a great cause. By learning we fit ourselves to contribute to the kingdom. Together we can build what no one can build alone.

I sincerely pray that the Lord will help us all to grow older gracefully, still vital and contributing and growing. I pray that He will help us develop that faith in Him that serves as the drive spring to good works. I pray that He will help us improve our talents, to equip ourselves for work in His cause. And I pray that we can fulfill our destiny as children of God, striving to be like Him, loving and serving His other children, and building Zion.

I do so in the name of Jesus Christ, amen.

"Many Things... One Thing"

PATRICIA TERRY HOLLAND

From my varied experience of listening to and speaking with many of our sisters, both younger and older, I know something of the struggles and the pain and the anxiety that concern women of our time. Every era has its problems. My limitations surely won't allow me to address every problem, anticipate every question, or meet every need, but I promise you two things. First, I promise you my love. You are my sisters and my friends. And second, I promise you my honesty. It's important to me that you know I speak from the honesty of my heart.

Our theme this year is unity of faith and diversity of works. That obviously suggests the unity and diversity among many women, but it also has an application within each individual woman — *her* unity and *her* diversity. For a moment may I speak of *woman* and see what significance it might have for *women*.

To do so, I must begin by being just a little autobiographical. Just after my release from the general presidency of the Young Women in April 1986, I had the opportunity of spending a week in Israel. It had been a very difficult and demanding two years for me. Being a good mother, with the ample amount of time needed to succeed at that task, had always been my first priority; so I had tried to be a full-time mother to a grade-schooler, a high-schooler beginning to date, and a son preparing for his mission. I had also tried to be a full-time wife to a staggeringly busy university president with all of the twenty-four-hours-a-day campus responsibility that can be required of

Patricia Terry Holland, educator, musician, and homemaker, served as first counselor in the Young Women General Presidency. She studied music and voice with a member of the faculty of the Juilliard School of Music in New York and also attended Dixie College and Brigham Young University. She and her husband, President Jeffrey R. Holland of BYU, have three children.

both of us at a place like Brigham Young University. And I had tried to be as much of a full-time counselor in that general presidency as one living fifty miles from the office could be. Sister Ardeth Kapp and the others were wonderfully patient with me. I will *never* be able to thank Ardeth enough. But in an important period of forming principles and starting programs for the Young Women, I worried that I wasn't doing enough—and I tried to run a little faster.

Toward the end of my two-year term, my health was going downhill. I was losing weight steadily and couldn't seem to do anything to halt that. Furthermore, I wasn't sleeping well. My husband and children were trying to bandage me together even as I was trying to do the same for them. We were exhausted. And yet, I kept wondering what I might have done to manage it all better. The Brethren, always compassionate, were watching and at the end of the two-year term extended a loving release. As grateful as my family and I were for the conclusion of my term of service, I nevertheless felt a loss of association—and, I confess, some loss of identity— with these women whom I had come to love so much. Who was I and where was I in this welter of demands? Should life be as hard as all this? How successful had I been in my several and competing assignments? Or had I muffed them all? The days after my release were about as difficult as the weeks before it. I didn't have any reserve to call on. My tank was on empty, and I wasn't sure there was a filling station anywhere in sight.

It was just a few weeks later that my husband had the assignment in Jerusalem to which I have referred, and the Brethren traveling on the assignment requested that I accompany him. "Come on," he said. "You can recuperate in the Savior's land of living water and bread of life." As weary as I was, I packed my bags, believing—or, at the very least, hoping— that the time there would be a healing respite.

On a pristinely clear and beautifully bright day, I sat overlooking the sea of Galilee and reread Luke 10:38. But instead of the words there on the page, I thought I saw with my mind and heard with my heart these words: "Pat, Pat, thou art careful and troubled about many things." Then the power of pure and

12

personal revelation seized me as I read, "But one thing [only one thing] is truly needful."

In Israel in May the sun is so bright that you feel as if you are sitting on top of the world. I had just visited the spot in Bethoron where the "sun stood still" for Joshua, and indeed on that day it seemed so for me as well. As I sat pondering my problems, I felt that same sun's healing rays like warm liquid pouring into my heart—relaxing, calming, and comforting my troubled soul. I found myself lifted to a higher view of my life.

Spirit to spirit, our loving Father in Heaven seemed to be whispering to me, "You don't have to worry over so many things. The one thing that is needful—the only thing that is truly needful—is to keep your eyes toward the sun—my Son." "Learn of me," he seemed to say, "and listen to my words; walk in the meekness of my Spirit, and you shall have peace in me." (D&C 19:23.) Suddenly I did have peace. I knew, as surely as I know you sit before me, that my life had always been in His hands—from the very beginning! And so are the lives of all of you, of every woman who wants to do right and grows in capacity and tries to give all she can. The sea lying peacefully before my very eyes had been tempest tossed and dangerous many, many times. All I needed to do was to renew my faith, get a firm grasp of His hand, and together we could walk on the water.

I had, for a few months, been pushed to my extremity, but that is always God's opportunity. I had learned so much, and yet now I was learning even more. The Son was enlightening my world. We all at one time or another find ourselves in the midst of a turbulent sea. There are times when we, too, would like to cry out, "Master, carest thou not that we perish?" I suppose it is for this very purpose that so many of us are drawn together today as women of faith, seeking solace and sisterly strength to carry us safely to drier and firmer ground.

I would like to pose a question for each of us to ponder. How do we as women make that quantum leap from being troubled and worried, including worries about legitimate concerns, to being women of even greater faith? One frame of mind surely seems to negate the other. Faith and fear cannot long coexist. While you think of faith and walking hand in hand with God, I would like to examine why I believe there are so many worries — "troubles," Luke 10 calls them — and to note some of the things we are legitimately worried about.

I have served as a Relief Society president in four different wards. Two of these wards were for single women, and two were traditional wards with many young mothers. As I sat in counsel with my single sisters, my heart often ached as they described to me their feelings of loneliness and disappointment. They felt that their lives had no meaning or purpose in a church that rightly puts so much emphasis on marriage and family life. Most painful of all was the occasional suggestion that their singleness was their own fault — or worse yet, a selfish desire. They were anxiously seeking for peace and purpose, something of real value to which they could give their lives.

Yet at the very same time, it seemed to me that the young mothers had easily as many concerns as they described to me the struggles of trying to raise children in an increasingly difficult world, of never having enough time or means or freedom to feel like a person of value because they were always stretched to the ragged edge of survival. And there were so few tangible evidences that what they were doing was really going to be successful. There was no one to give them a raise in pay, and beyond their husbands (who may or may not have remembered to do it), no one to compliment them on a job well done. And they were always tired! The one thing I remember so vividly with these young mothers was that they were always so tired.

Then there were those women who through no fault of their own found themselves the sole provider for their families financially, spiritually, emotionally, and in every other way. I could not even comprehend the challenges they faced. Obviously, in some ways theirs was the most demanding circumstance of all.

The perspective I have gained over these many years of listening to the worries of women is that no one woman or group of women — single, married, divorced, or widowed, homemakers or professionals — has cornered the full market

14

on concerns. There seems to be plenty of challenges to go around. And, I hasten to add, marvelous blessings as well. In this, too, we are united in our diversity. Every one of us does have privileges and blessings, and we do have fears and trials. Some of these fears, anxieties, and worries have been pointed out to me from those of you who met with us at this conference last year. A partial list taken from the evaluation sheets you filled out one year ago notes concerns ranging from loneliness to raising children to inactive husbands to physical health and self-esteem.

The complete, longer list is staggering! It seems bold to say, but common sense suggests, that never before in the history of the world have women, including Latter-day Saint women, been faced with greater complexity in their concerns.

In addressing these concerns I am very appreciative of the added awareness that the women's movement has given to a gospel principle we have had since Mother Eve and before — that of free agency, the right to choose.

But one of the most unfortunate side effects we have faced in this matter of agency is, because of the increasing diversity of life-styles for women of today, we seem even more uncertain and less secure with each other. We are getting not closer but further away from that sense of community and sisterhood that has sustained us and given us unique strength for generations. There seems to be an increase in our competitiveness and a decrease in our generosity with one another.

Those who have the time and energy to can their fruit and vegetables develop a great skill that will serve them well in time of need — and in our uncertain economic times, that could be almost any day of the week. But they shouldn't look down their noses at those who buy their peaches, or who don't like zucchini in any of the thirty-five ways there are to disguise it, or who have simply made a conscious choice to use their time and energy in some other purposeful way.

And where am I in all of this? For three-fourths of my life I was threatened to the core because I hated to sew. Now I *can* sew; if absolutely forced to, I *will* sew — but I hate it. Imagine my burden over the last twenty-five or thirty years, faking it in Relief Society sessions and trying to smile when six little girls walk into church all pinafored and laced and ribboned and petticoated — identical, hand sewn — all trooping ahead of their mother, who has the same immaculate outfit. Competitive? I wanted to tear their pleats out.

I don't necessarily consider it virtuous, lovely, or of good report, or praiseworthy — but I'm honest in my antipathy toward sewing. If even one sister out there is weeping tears of relief, then I consider my public shame at least a partial blow against stereotyping. I have grown up a little since those days in at least two ways — I now genuinely admire a mother who can do that for her children, and I have ceased feeling guilty that sewing is not particularly rewarding to me.

We simply cannot call ourselves Christian and continue to judge one another — or ourselves — so harshly. No Mason jar of Bing cherries is worth a confrontation that robs us of our compassion and our sisterhood.

Obviously the Lord has created us with different personalities, as well as differing degrees of energy, interest, health, talent, and opportunity. So long as we are committed to righteousness and living a life of faithful devotion, we should celebrate these divine differences, knowing they are a gift from God. We must not feel so frightened; we must not be so threatened and insecure; we must not need to find exact replicas of ourselves in order to feel validated as women of worth. There are many things over which we can be divided, but one thing is needful for our unity — the empathy and compassion of the living Son of God.

I was married in 1963, the very year Betty Friedan published her society-shaking book, *The Feminine Mystique*, so as an adult woman I can look back with only childhood memories of the gentler forties and fifties. But it must have been much more comfortable to have a pattern already prepared for you and neighbors on either side whose lives gave you role models for your own; however, it must have been even that much more painful for those who, through no fault of their own, were single then, or who had to work, or who struggled with a broken family. Now, with our increasingly complex world, even that earlier model is torn, and we seem to be even less sure of who we are and where we are going.

Surely, there has not been another time in history in which women have questioned their self-worth as harshly and critically as in the second half of the twentieth century. Many women are searching, almost frantically, as never before, for a sense of personal purpose and meaning—and many LDS women are searching, too, for eternal insight and meaning—in their femaleness.

If I were Satan and wanted to destroy a society, I think I too would stage a full-blown blitz on its women. I would keep them so distraught and distracted that they would never find the calming strength and serenity for which their sex has always been known. He has effectively done that, catching us in the crunch of trying to be superhuman instead of realistically striving to reach our individual purpose and unique God-given potential within such diversity. He tauntingly teases us that if we don't have it all—fame, fortune, families, and fun, and have it every minute all the time—we have been short-changed; we are second-class citizens in the race of life. You'd have to be deaf, dumb, and blind not to get these messages in today's world, and as a sex we are struggling, our families are struggling, and our society struggles. Drugs, teenage pregnancies, divorce, family violence, and suicide are some of the ever-increasing side effects of our collective life in the express lane.

As a result, we are experiencing new and undiagnosed stress-related illnesses. The Epstein-Barr syndrome, for one, has come into our popular medical jargon as the malady of the eighties. Its symptoms are low-grade fevers, aching joints, and other flulike symptoms—but it isn't the flu. It carries with it overwhelming exhaustion, muscular weakness, and physical debilitations—but it isn't the dreaded AIDS. Its victims are often confused and forgetful; but, no, it isn't Alzheimer's. Many feel suicidal, but this disease lacks the traditional characteristics of clinical depression. And yes, it can strike men, but three times out of four it doesn't. This illness is primarily a woman's disease, and those most vulnerable are the so-called "fast-track" women in high-stress, conflicting roles. (*Newsweek,* 27 Oct. 1986.)

When I recently mentioned this to the young women in our BYU student body, I was flooded with telephone calls and letters saying, "I have it! I have it! I must have Epstein-Barr!" Well, whether they do or do not, I can't say. But the body and its immune system are affected by stress. Those calls and letters tell me that too many are struggling and suffering; too many are running faster than they have strength, expecting too much of themselves. We must have the courage to be imperfect while striving for perfection. We must not allow our own guilt or the feminist books, the talk-show hosts or the whole media culture to sell us a bill of goods — or rather, a bill of no goods.

I believe we can become so sidetracked in our compulsive search for identity and self-esteem and self-awareness that we really believe it can be found in having perfect figures or academic degrees or professional status or even absolute motherly success. Yet in so searching externally, we can be torn from our true internal, eternal selves. We often worry so much about pleasing and performing for others that we lose our own uniqueness — that full and relaxed acceptance of ourselves as persons of worth and individuality. We become so frightened and insecure that we cannot be generous toward the diversity and the individuality and, yes, the problems, of our neighbors. Too many women with these anxieties watch helplessly as their lives unravel from the very core that centers and sustains them. Too many are like a ship at sea without sail or rudder, tossed to and fro (as the Apostle Paul said) until more and more are genuinely, rail-grabbingly seasick.

Where is the sureness that allows us to sail our ship whatever winds may blow — with the master seaman's triumphant cry, "Steady as she goes"? Where is the inner stillness we so cherish and for which our sex traditionally has been known?

I believe we can find it — the steady footing and the stilling of the soul — by turning away from the fragmentation of physical preoccupations, or superwoman accomplishments, or endless popularity contests and returning instead to the wholeness of our soul, that unity in our very being that balances the demanding and inevitable diversity of life.

One woman who is not of our faith but whose writings I love is Anne Morrow Lindbergh. In commenting on the female despair and general torment of our times, she writes: "The Feminists did not look . . . far [enough] ahead; they laid down no rules of conduct. For them it was enough to demand the privileges. . . . And [so] woman today is still searching. We are aware of our hunger and needs, but still ignorant of what will satisfy them. With our garnered free time, we are more apt to drain our creative springs than to refill them. With our pitchers, we attempt . . . to water a field, [instead of] a garden. We throw ourselves indiscriminately into committees and causes. Not knowing how to free the spirit, we try to muffle its demands in distractions. Instead of stilling the center, the axis of the wheel, we add more centrifugal activities to our lives—which tend to throw us [yet more] off balance.

"Mechanically we have gained, in the last generation, but spiritually we have . . . lost. . . .

"[For women] the problem is [still] how to feed the soul." (*Gift from the Sea*, 20th anniversary edition, with an afterword by the author [New York: Vintage Books, 1978], pp. 52 and 51, respectively.)

I have pondered long and hard about the feeding of our inner self, of the "one thing needful" amidst too many troublesome things. It is no coincidence that we speak of "feeding the spirit" just as we would speak of feeding the body. We need constant nourishment for both. The root word *hale* (as in "hale and hearty") is the common root to words like *whole, health, heal,* and *holy.* President Ezra Taft Benson recently said on this campus, "There is no question that the health of the body affects the spirit, or the Lord would never have revealed the Word of Wisdom. God has never given any *temporal* commandments—and that which affects our stature affects our soul." We need so much for body, mind, and spirit to come together, to unite in one healthy, stable soul.

Surely God is well balanced, so perhaps we are just that much closer to Him when we are. In any case, I like the link between *hale, whole, health, heal,* and *holy.* Our unity of soul within diversity of circumstance—our "stilling of the center"—

is worth the effort of this conference and anything else that may encourage it.

As I noted previously, I believe we make too many external quests seeking peace or fulfillment. Only rarely do we consider the glorious possibility within us, within our own souls. We seem never to remember that divine promise, "The kingdom of God is within you." (Luke 17:21.) Perhaps we forget that the Kingdom of God is within us because too much attention is given to the Kingdom of Women outside us, this outer shell, this human body of ours, and the frail, too-flimsy world in which it moves. So, as women of faith, we should make an inward quest.

In my contribution to this effort, may I share with you an expanded version of an analogy that I shared with the students at the beginning of their winter semester. It is my own analogy of something I read years ago, a process that helped me then — and helps me still — in my examination of inner strength and spiritual growth.

The analogy is of a soul — a human soul, with all of its splendor — being placed in a beautifully carved but very tightly locked box. Reigning in majesty and illuminating our soul in this innermost box is our Lord and our Redeemer, Jesus Christ, the living Son of the living God. This box is then placed — and locked — inside another larger one, and so on until five beautifully carved but very securely locked boxes await the woman who is skillful and wise enough to open them. In order for her to have free communication with the Lord she must find the key to these boxes and unlock their contents. Success will then reveal to her the beauty and divinity of her own soul, her gifts and her grace as a daughter of God.

For me, prayer is the key to the first box. We kneel to ask help for the tasks and then arise to find that the first lock is now open. But this ought not to seem just a convenient and contrived miracle. No, if we are to search for real light and eternal certainties, we have to pray as the ancients prayed. We are women now, not children, and are expected to pray with maturity. The words most often used to describe urgent, prayerful labor are *wrestle, plead, cry,* and *hunger.* In some sense, prayer may be the hardest work we will ever be engaged in, and perhaps it should be. We sing, "Prayer is the soul's sincere desire," our most basic declaration that we have no other God before us. It is our most pivotal protection against overinvolvement in worldly things and becoming so absorbed with possessions and privilege and honors and status that we no longer desire to undertake the search for our soul.

For those who, like Enos, pray in faith and gain entrance to a new dimension of their divinity, they are led to box number two. Here our prayers alone do not seem to be sufficient. We must turn to the scriptures for God's long-recorded teachings about our soul. We must learn. Surely every woman in this Church is under divine obligation to learn and grow and develop. We are God's diverse array of unburnished talents, and we must not bury these gifts nor hide our light. If the glory of God is intelligence, then learning stretches us toward Him, especially learning from the scriptures. There He uses many metaphors for divine influence, such as "living water" and "the bread of life." I have discovered that if my own progress stalls, it stalls from malnutrition, born of not eating and drinking daily from His holy writ. There have been challenges in my life that would have completely destroyed me, would have precluded any spiritual progression at all, had I not had a copy of the scriptures by my bed and a small set in my purse so that I could partake of them day and night at a moment's notice. Meeting God in scripture has been like a divine intravenous feeding for me — a celestial I.V. that my son once described as an "angelical" cord. So box two is opened spirit to spirit through the scriptures. I have discovered that by opening them I have opened it. There I can have, again and again, an exhilarating encounter with God.

At the beginning of such success in emancipating the soul, however, Lucifer becomes more anxious, especially as we approach box number three. He knows something is coming, one very important and fundamental principle. He knows that we are about to learn that to truly find ourselves we must lose ourselves, so he begins to block our increased efforts to love — love God, love our neighbor, and love ourselves. Remember, the Lord has asked above all else that we love. Everything else we do is secondary, and in fulfilling the two great commandments, we can often measure how much we love the Lord by how well we truly love our neighbor. I firmly believe that if we did nothing else but faithfully practice love for our neighbor, we would have found our ability and success in accomplishing all else. Yet Satan's skillful deception has been to obscure this chance for near success. He has, especially in the last decade, enticed the world to engage so much of their energies in the pursuit of romantic love or thing-love or excessive self-love. In so doing we can forget that appropriate self-love and self-esteem are the promised reward for putting other things first. "Whosoever shall seek to save his life shall lose it; and whosoever shall lose his life shall preserve it." (Luke 17:33.) Box three opens only with the key of charity.

Real growth and genuine insight are coming now. But the lid to box four seems nearly impossible to penetrate, for we are climbing, too, in this story, and the way inward is also the way upward. Unfortunately the faint-hearted and fearful often turn back here—the going seems too difficult, the lock too secure. This is a time for self-evaluation. To see ourselves as we really are often brings pain, but it is only through true humility that we will come to know God. "Learn of me; for I am meek and lowly of heart." (Matthew 11:29.) We must be patient with ourselves as we overcome weaknesses, and we must remember to rejoice over all that is good in us. This will strengthen the inner woman and leave her less dependent on outward acclaim. When the soul reaches the stage where it pays less attention to praise, it then also cares very little when the public disapproves. Comparing and competition and jealousy and envy begin to have no meaning now. Just imagine the powerful spirit that would exist in our female society if we finally arrived at the point where, like our Savior, our real desire was to be counted as the least among our sisters. The rewards here are of such profound strength and quiet triumph of faith that we are carried into an even brighter sphere. So the fourth box, unlike the others, is broken open, as a heart and contrite spirit are broken. Or better yet, it bursts open as a flower blooms and the earth is reborn. We are reborn, too, in humility and repentance and renewal. We are born of water and of fire. We are born of the Spirit of God.

To share with you my feelings of opening the fifth box, I must compare the beauty of our souls with the holiness of our temples. There, in a setting not of this world, in a place where fashions and position and professions go unrecognized, we have our chance to meet God face to face. For those who, like the brother of Jared, have the courage and faith to break through the veil into that sacred center of existence, we will find the brightness of the final box brighter than the noonday sun. There we will find peace and serenity and stillness that will anchor our soul forever, for there we will find God. Wholeness. Holiness. That is what it says over the entrance to the fifth box: "Holiness to the Lord." "Know ye not that ye are the temple of God?" (1 Corinthians 3:16.) I testify that you are holy — that divinity is abiding within you waiting to be uncovered — to be unleashed and magnified and demonstrated.

I believe that if any woman is to find her own personal identity and value for herself, her family, her society, and her God, she will have to uncover her own soul and set it free. Then it can and should range throughout all eternity, having great influence and doing much good.

As I conclude, I pray for a special spirit to be with me so that I might articulate what I have recently been feeling about this whole matter of identity — the eternal identity of our womanhood. These thoughts are my own, and I take full responsibility for them. Above all, I do not want them to be misunderstood nor to give offense.

I have heard it said by some that the reason women in the Church struggle somewhat to know themselves is that they don't have a divine female role model. But we do believe we have a Mother in Heaven. May I quote from President Spencer W. Kimball in a general conference address: "When we sing that doctrinal hymn ... 'O My Father,' we get a sense of the ultimate in maternal modesty, of the restrained, queenly elegance of our heavenly mother, and, knowing how profoundly our mortal mothers have shaped us here, do we suppose her influence on us as individuals to be less?" (*Ensign,* May 1978, p. 4.)

I have never questioned why our Mother in Heaven seems veiled to us, for I believe the Lord has His reasons for revealing as little as He has on that subject. Furthermore, I believe we know much more about our eternal nature than we think we do; and it is our sacred obligation to identify it and to teach it to our young sisters and daughters, and in so doing, strengthen their faith and help them through the counterfeit confusions of these difficult latter days. Let me point out some examples.

The Lord has not placed us in this lone and dreary world without a blueprint for living. In Doctrine and Covenants 52:14 we read, "And again, I will give unto you a pattern in *all things, that ye may not be deceived.*" (Italics added.) He certainly includes us as women in that promise. He has given us patterns in the Bible, the Book of Mormon, the Doctrine and Covenants, the Pearl of Great Price; and He has given us patterns in the temple ceremony. As we study these patterns we must continually ask, "Why does the Lord choose to say these particular words and present it in just this way?" We know He uses metaphors and symbols and parables and allegories to teach us of His eternal ways. For example, we all have recognized the relationship between Abraham and Isaac that so parallels God's anguish over the sacrifice of His son, Jesus Christ. But, as women, do we stretch ourselves and also ask about Sarah's travail in this experience as well? We could, and if we did, I believe we would learn. We need to search, and we need always to look for deeper meaning. We should look for parallels and symbols. We should look for themes and motifs just as we would in a Bach or a Mozart composition, and we should look for patterns—repeated patterns—in the gospel. One obvious pattern is that both the Bible and the Book of Mormon start off with family, including family conflict. I have always believed that symbolized something eternal about all of us as "family" far more than the story of just those particular parents or those particular children. Surely all of us—married or single, with children and without—see something of Adam and Eve and something of Cain and Abel every day of our lives. With or without marriage or with or without children, surely we have some of the feelings of Lehi, Sariah, Laman, Nephi, Ruth, Naomi, Esther, the sons of Helaman, and the daughters of Ishmael.

Those are types and shadows for us, prefigurations of our own mortal joys and sorrows, just as Joseph and Mary are, in a sense, types and shadows of parental devotion as they nurtured the Son of God Himself, with Mary playing the principal mortal role. These all seem to me to be symbols of higher principles and truths, symbols carefully chosen to show us the way, whether we are married or single, young or old, with family or without.

And obviously the temple is highly symbolic. May I share an experience I had there a few months ago? It has to do with the careful choice of words and symbols. I have chosen my own words carefully so that nothing I say will be improperly shared outside the temple. My only quotations are taken from published scripture.

Maybe it was coincidence, but as someone has said, "Coincidence is a small miracle in which God chooses to remain anonymous." In any case, as I waited in the temple chapel, I sat next to a very elderly man who unexpectedly but sweetly turned to me and said, "If you want a clear picture of the Creation, read Abraham, chapter 4." As I started to turn to Abraham, I just happened to brush past Moses 3:5: "For I, the Lord God, created all things, of which I have spoken, spiritually, before they were naturally upon the face of the earth." Another message of prefiguration again—a spiritual pattern giving meaning to mortal creations. I then read Abraham 4 carefully and took the opportunity of going to an initiatory session. I left there with greater revelatory light on something I'd always known in my heart to be so—that men and women are joint heirs of the blessings of the priesthood and, even though men bear the greater burden of administering it, women are not without their priesthood-related responsibilities also.

Then as I attended the endowment session, I asked myself if I were the Lord and could give my children on earth only a simplified but powerfully symbolic example of their roles and missions, how much would I give and where would I start? I listened to every word. I watched for patterns and prototypes.

I quote to you from Abraham 4:27: "So the Gods went down to organize man in their own image, in the image of the Gods to form they him, male *and* female to form they *them.*" (Italics added.) They formed male, and they formed female— in the image of the Gods, in Their own image.

Then in a poignant exchange with God, Adam states that he will call the woman "Eve." And why does he call her Eve? "Because she was the mother of all living." (Genesis 3:20; Moses 4:26.)

As I tenderly acknowledge the very real pain that many single women, or married women who have not borne children, feel about any discussion of motherhood, could we consider this one possibility about our eternal female identity— our unity in our diversity. Eve was given the identity of the mother of all living—years, decades, perhaps centuries before she had ever borne a child. It would appear that her motherhood preceded her maternity just as surely as the perfection of the Garden preceded the struggles of mortality. I believe *mother* is one of those very carefully chosen words, one of those words rich with meaning after meaning after meaning. We must not, at all costs, let that word divide us. I believe with all my heart that it is first and foremost a statement about our nature, not a head count of our children. I have only three children and have wept that I could not have eight. (Some of you have eight and weep that you can't have three.) And I know that some of you without any have wept, too. And sometimes, too many have simply been angry over the very subject itself. For the sake of our eternal motherhood I plead that this not be so. Some women give birth and raise children but never "mother" them. Others, whom I love with all my heart, "mother" all their lives but have never given birth. Therefore, we must understand that however we accomplish it, parenthood is the highest of callings, the holiest of assignments. And all of us are Eve's daughters, married or single, maternal or barren, every one of us. We are created in the image of the Gods to become Gods and Goddesses. And we can provide something of that divine pattern, that maternal prototype for each other and for those who come after us. Whatever our circumstance, we can reach out, touch, hold, lift, and nurture — but we cannot do it in isolation. We need a community of sisters stilling the soul and binding the wounds of fragmentation.

I know that God loves us individually and collectively — as women — and that He has a personal mission, an individual purpose for every one of us. As I learned on my Galilean hillside, I testify that if our desires are righteous, God overrules for our good, and Heavenly Parents will tenderly attend to our needs. In our diversity and individuality, my prayer is that we will be united — united in seeking our specific, foreordained mission, united in asking, not "What can the Kingdom do for me?" but "What can I do for the Kingdom? How do I fulfill the measure of *my* creation? In my circumstances and my challenges and with my faith, where is my *full* realization of the godly image in which I was created?"

With faith in God, His prophets, His Church, and ourselves — faith in our own divine creation — may we be peaceful and let go of our cares and troubles over so many things. May we believe — nothing doubting — in the light that shines, even in a dark place.

Your presence here today (in all your diversity) is evidence that you are women of faith. We have gathered today in the warmth and beauty of the renewing sun (Son) of spring, just as the multitudes gathered at His feet in Galilee. We are His disciples. He accepts us as we are, even as we are growing toward what we must become. Rest in that love. Bathe and luxuriate in it. Let it relax, calm, and comfort you. Let us keep our face to the Son and come unto Him. "Listen to my words," He counseled us. "Walk in the meekness of my Spirit, and you shall have peace in me." (D&C 19:23.)

Spiritual Gifts

ELDER DALLIN H. OAKS

*F*aith is a spiritual gift. So is personal revelation. So is a testimony of Jesus Christ. And there are other spiritual gifts.

We know too little about spiritual gifts. This is evident in our communications, and it is also evident in our failure to seek after and use spiritual gifts.

It is important to understand the relationship between spiritual gifts and the Spirit of Christ, manifestations of the Holy Ghost, and the gift of the Holy Ghost.

Moroni says that all spiritual gifts "come by the Spirit of Christ." (Moroni 10:17.) The Spirit of Christ "giveth light to every man that cometh into the world." (D&C 84:46.) It "is given to every man, that he may know good from evil." (Moroni 7:16.) By this means every son and daughter of God has "the light" to judge what is right, and to seek to "lay hold upon every good thing." (Moroni 7:18–19.) By this Spirit, all may seek to learn of God and to exercise faith in Him. Enlightened by this Spirit, all may seek spiritual gifts, which, Moroni says, "come unto every man severally, according as he will." (Moroni 10:17.)

While the Spirit of Christ is the means by which spiritual gifts are transmitted to men and women, such gifts come by the power of the Holy Ghost, as I will explain later.

The Holy Ghost testifies of Jesus Christ (see John 15:26; 1 Corinthians 12:3; 1 Nephi 31:18) and leads us into all truth

Elder Dallin H. Oaks is a member of the Quorum of the Twelve Apostles. Before his calling as an apostle in April 1984, he had served for more than three years as a justice of the Utah Supreme Court, for five years as the chairman of the board of the Public Broadcasting Service, for nine years as president of Brigham Young University, and for ten years as professor of law at the University of Chicago Law School. He received his B.A. from BYU and his J.D. from the University of Chicago Law School. He and his wife, June Dixon Oaks, are the parents of six children and the grandparents of sixteen.

(see John 16:13; Moroni 10:4–5; D&C 45:57). We need to distinguish between a *manifestation* of the Holy Ghost and the *gift* of the Holy Ghost.

As men and women desire to believe, they develop faith in God. (See Alma 32:26–43.) When they have enough faith, they can receive a manifestation of the Holy Ghost. In unusual circumstances, to serve the purposes of God, such a manifestation might even include seeing heavenly beings. The Book of Mormon has such an account.

Ammon preached to the wicked King Lamoni. When the king believed and cried to the Lord for mercy, he fell to the earth as if he were dead. (See Alma 18:22–43.) After two days Lamoni's people were about to bury him, but the queen, hearing that Ammon was a prophet, called for him and asked him what she should do. Ammon told her the king would revive on the morrow. The queen believed him, and Ammon called her blessed because of her "exceeding faith." (Alma 19:10.)

When King Lamoni arose, he blessed the name of God and prophesied that the Redeemer would be born of a woman and would redeem all mankind who believed on His name. Afterwards, he and the queen and Ammon sank down, overpowered by the Spirit. After the people had assembled, the queen arose first. She "cried with a loud voice, saying: O blessed Jesus, who has saved me from an awful hell! O blessed God, have mercy upon this people!" Ammon baptized King Lamoni, the queen and many of their people. (See Alma 19:12–35.)

Here we see the power and witness of the Holy Ghost poured out upon a woman and a man who had not yet been baptized. After they and their followers were converted by this witness, they were baptized and received the *gift* of the Holy Ghost. Then, as the scripture records, "they became a righteous people" and "the Lord did begin to pour out his Spirit upon them." (Alma 19:35–36.)

In summary, the Spirit of Christ is given to all men and women that they may know good from evil, and manifestations of the Holy Ghost are given to lead earnest seekers to repentance and baptism. These are preparatory gifts. What we term *spiritual gifts* come next.

Spiritual gifts come to those who have received the gift of the Holy Ghost. As the Prophet Joseph Smith taught, the gifts of the Spirit "are obtained through that medium" [the Holy Ghost] and "cannot be enjoyed without the gift of the Holy Ghost. . . . The world in general can know nothing about them." (*Teachings of the Prophet Joseph Smith,* comp. Joseph Fielding Smith [Salt Lake City: Deseret Book Co., 1938], pp. 243, 245; see also Elder Marion G. Romney, in Conference Report, Apr. 1956, p. 72.)

The gift of the Holy Ghost is conferred on both men and women. So are spiritual gifts. As Elder Bruce R. McConkie declared in Nauvoo at the dedication of the Monument to Women: "Where spiritual things are concerned, as pertaining to all of the gifts of the Spirit, with reference to the receipt of revelation, the gaining of testimonies, and the seeing of visions, in all matters that pertain to godliness and holiness and which are brought to pass as a result of personal righteousness—in all these things men and women stand in a position of absolute equality before the Lord. He is no respecter of persons nor of sexes, and he blesses those men and those women who seek him and serve him and keep his commandments." (*Ensign,* Jan. 1979, p. 61.)

Spiritual gifts do not come visibly, automatically, and immediately to all who have received the gift of the Holy Ghost. The Prophet Joseph Smith taught that most such gifts are "not visible to the natural vision, or understanding of man," and that it "require[s] time and circumstances to call these gifts into operation." (*Teachings,* pp. 244, 246.)

The scriptures tell us that we should desire and zealously seek spiritual gifts. (See D&C 46:8; 1 Corinthians 12:31; 14:1, 11.) We are also told that some will receive one gift and some will receive another. (See D&C 46:11; 1 Corinthians 12; Moroni 10:8–18.) In every case, the receipt of spiritual gifts is predicated upon faith, obedience, and personal righteousness. (See Bruce R. McConkie, *A New Witness for the Articles of Faith* [Salt Lake City: Deseret Book Co., 1985], p. 367.)

Spiritual gifts are evidently among the "signs [that] shall follow them that believe." (Mark 16:17; see also McConkie, *New Witness,* p. 366.)

We are commanded not to seek for signs to develop our faith (see Matthew 12:39; D&C 63:12), for "faith cometh not by signs" (D&C 63:9). But when we have faith, repent, and are born of water and the Spirit, and when we love and serve God with all our hearts, we are eligible to receive spiritual gifts. We may then, as Paul taught, "covet earnestly [which means fervently desire] the best gifts." (1 Corinthians 12:31; see also D&C 46:8.)

When we believe and seek spiritual gifts to benefit others "and not for a sign" (D&C 46:9), we are told that signs will follow. "Behold, . . . signs follow those that believe. Yea, signs come by faith, not by the will of men, nor as they please, but by the will of God. Yea, signs come by faith, unto mighty works." (D&C 63:9–11.) The Holy Ghost "maketh manifest unto the children of men, according to their faith." (Jarom 1:4.)

Let us consider some of these spiritual gifts.

Faith is a gift of the Spirit. (See Moroni 10:11; 1 Corinthians 12:9.) As Alma taught, this gift takes root in our hearts as hope and, nurtured as a seedling, will eventually flower as knowledge and bear the fruit of eternal life. (See Alma 32:26–43.)

Another familiar spiritual gift is the gift of testimony. "To some it is given by the Holy Ghost to know that Jesus Christ is the Son of God, and that He was crucified for the sins of the world." (D&C 46:13; see also Moroni 10:7; 1 Corinthians 12:3.) Many Latter-day Saints have this gift.

Others have a related gift, as shown by these two verses in section 46 of the Doctrine and Covenants: "To some it is given by the Holy Ghost to know that Jesus Christ is the Son of God. . . . To others it is given to believe on their words, that they also might have eternal life if they continue faithful." (D&C 46:13–14.)

Where it is given to some to know and to others to believe on their words, those who know must be responsible for sharing their testimonies. Only in this way can they give those who have the gift of believing on their words something to lean upon as they, too, move toward eternal life.

The relationship between these gifts illustrates the purpose for which all spiritual gifts are given: "And all these gifts come from God, for the benefit of the children of God." (V. 26.) Spiritual gifts are given to members of the Church "that all may be profited thereby." (D&C 46:12; see also D&C 46:9; Moroni 10:8.) The same principle is evident in Paul's teachings in 1 Corinthians 12. Here spiritual gifts are likened to the various parts of the body, each performing its own function and each serving the entire "body of Christ." (V. 27.)

We must take care never to misuse spiritual gifts. As the Prophet Joseph Smith taught, when spiritual gifts "are applied to that which God does not intend, they prove an injury, a snare and a curse instead of a blessing." (*Teachings*, p. 248.)

Another spiritual gift is the gift of "teach[ing] the word of knowledge by the same Spirit." (Moroni 10:10; see also Alma 9:21; D&C 46:18.) Many of us have received this gift, and we have all been blessed by its exercise.

The spiritual gift referred to as the "word of wisdom" (see D&C 46:17; Moroni 10:9; 1 Corinthians 12:8) has been explained as the wise application of knowledge. I would call this *judgment*. This is a precious gift for any field of knowledge, but judgment in applying spiritual knowledge is a quality of eternal worth.

To others are given the gifts of speaking with tongues or interpreting tongues. (See D&C 46:24–25; Moroni 10:15–16; 1 Corinthians 12:10.) These two gifts should always be manifest together because the purpose of spiritual gifts having to do with communication is to edify the people of God. (See Marion G. Romney, in Conference Report, Apr. 1956, p. 71.) If a person spoke in tongues without someone to interpret, there would be no edification. This is why the Prophet Joseph Smith taught that members should not "speak in tongues except there be an interpreter present." (*Teachings*, p. 247; see also 1 Corinthians 14:28.)

To others is given the gift of "faith to be healed." (D&C 46:19.) Most of us know persons who have been healed miraculously. Many of these healings are attributable, at least in part, to their gift of faith to be healed.

Another spiritual gift is "faith to heal." (D&C 46:20; see also Moroni 10:11; 1 Corinthians 12:9; *Teachings*, pp. 224–25.)

This gift has an obvious relationship to priesthood administration to the sick. It has additional significance as well, since both men and women can pray for and exercise faith that a loved one will be healed. The Apostle James taught the early Saints: "Pray for one another, that ye may be healed. The effectual fervent prayer of a righteous man availeth much." (James 5:16.)

The Bible tells us that if there are any sick among us we should "call for the elders of the Church" who should pray over them, anointing them with oil in the name of the Lord, "and the prayer of faith shall save the sick, and the Lord shall raise him up." (James 5:14–15.) Similarly, the Doctrine and Covenants states that the elders shall be called to "pray for and lay their hands upon [the sick]" in the name of the Lord, and "he that hath faith . . . to be healed, and is not appointed unto death, shall be healed." (D&C 42:44, 48.) These scriptures obviously refer to administrations to the sick by those who hold the priesthood, but they also stress the importance of faith in the performance and receipt of that priesthood function.

The mingling of priesthood powers and spiritual gifts is also evident in another spiritual gift. "And again, to some is given the working of miracles." (D&C 46:21; see also Moroni 10:12; 1 Corinthians 12:10.) Miracles are obviously worked through the power of the priesthood, but the prayer of faith is also at work. The great sermon on faith in the twelfth chapter of Ether states: "For if there be no faith among the children of men God can do no miracle among them." (V. 12.) The working of miracles is described as a spiritual gift.

Since spiritual gifts come by the power of the Holy Ghost, and the gift of the Holy Ghost comes by the laying on of hands by those holding the priesthood, the priesthood is always a factor in spiritual gifts. But spiritual gifts obviously bless the lives of those who do not themselves hold the priesthood.

Moroni speaks of the spiritual gift of "beholding of angels and ministering spirits." (Moroni 10:14.) Alma and Amaleki both list this among the various gifts of the Spirit. (See Alma 9:21; Omni 1:25.) Mary had such an experience when she was visited by the angel who told her that she was to become the mother of the Son of God. (See Luke 1:26–38.)

A more familiar gift of the Spirit is personal revelation. Alma described the universal character of this spiritual gift: "And now, he imparteth his word by angels unto men, yea, not only men but women also. Now this is not all; little children do have words given unto them many times, which confound the wise and the learned." (Alma 32:23.)

There is a choice example of personal revelation in the twenty-fifth chapter of Genesis. When Rebekah was carrying the twins Jacob and Esau, "the children struggled together within her." The scripture says she was troubled at this and so "she went to enquire of the Lord." (Genesis 25:22.) Here we see a major principle of revelation. It usually comes in response to earnest prayer. "Ask, and it shall be given you; seek, and ye shall find; knock, and it shall be opened unto you." (Matthew 7:7.)

In this instance the Lord spoke to Rebekah, saying: "Two nations are in thy womb, and two manner of people shall be separated from thy bowels; and one people shall be stronger than the other people; and the elder shall serve the younger." (Genesis 25:23.) Though she was the wife of a prophet and patriarch, Rebekah inquired of the Lord and the Lord instructed her directly on a matter of great personal concern to her, to the children she would bear, and to generations unborn. After recounting this incident, Elder Bruce R. McConkie concluded: "The Lord gives revelation to women who pray to him in faith." (*New Era*, May 1978, p. 36.)

Another spiritual gift is the gift of prophecy. "And to others it is given to prophesy." (D&C 46:22; see also Moroni 10:13; 1 Corinthians 12:10; 14:1.)

The Bible has many references to women who had or will have the gift of prophecy. One of the clearest of these is from the sermon Peter preached on the Day of Pentecost. Relying on a prophecy from the Old Testament (see Joel 2:28–29), he declared:

"And it shall come to pass in the last days, saith God, I will pour out of my Spirit upon all flesh: and your sons and your daughters shall prophesy, and your young men shall see visions, and your old men shall dream dreams:

"And on my servants and on my handmaidens I will pour out in those days of my Spirit; and they shall prophesy." (Acts 2:17–18.)

The book of Acts states that four daughters of Phillip were blessed with the gift of prophecy. (See Acts 21:8–9.) One of the two mortal witnesses of the divinity of the infant Jesus was the aged woman, Anna. She was a holy woman who "departed not from the temple, but served God with fastings and prayers night and day." (Luke 2:37.) When Anna saw the infant Jesus in the temple, she gave thanks to the Lord and "spake of him to all them that looked for redemption in Jerusalem." (V. 38.) This is a classic illustration of prophetic testimony and utterance.

The Inspired Translation of the Old Testament contains a prophetic utterance by our first mother, Eve. (See Joseph Smith Translation, Genesis 4:11; Moses 5:11; see also references to prophecy by other women in Numbers 12:2; Judges 4:4.)

How can a woman have the gift of prophecy when she does not hold the priesthood? That question has confused some, because the nouns *prophecy* and *prophet* and their variations, such as the adjective *prophetic* and the verb *prophesy*, are used in several different senses.

When we hear the word *prophet* in our day, we are accustomed to think of *the* prophet. These words signify him who holds the prophetic *office* and is sustained as *the* prophet, seer, and revelator. The priesthood offices and powers exercised by the President of the Church are unique. As we learn in the Doctrine and Covenants, it is given to him to have "all the gifts of God which he bestows upon the heads of the church." (D&C 107:92; see also D&C 46:29; 50:26–28.)

The spiritual gift of prophecy is quite different. As we read in the Book of Revelation, "The testimony of Jesus is the spirit of prophecy." (Revelation 19:10.) The Prophet Joseph Smith relied on this scripture in teaching that "every other man who has the testimony of Jesus" is a prophet. (*Teachings,* p. 119.) Similarly, the Apostle Paul states that "he that prophesieth speaketh unto men to edification, and exhortation, and comfort." (1 Corinthians 14:3.) Thus, in the sense used in speaking of spiritual gifts, a prophet is one who testifies of Jesus Christ, teaches God's word, and exhorts God's people. In its scriptural sense, to prophesy means much more than to predict the future.

The scriptures often use the word *prophet* and its derivatives in the broad sense of one who teaches and testifies of God. When the prophet Moses was asked to forbid two men who "prophesied in the camp," he refused, expressing the wish "that all the Lord's people were prophets." (Numbers 11:26, 29.) The Apostle Paul taught that Christians should "desire spiritual gifts, but rather that ye may prophesy." (1 Corinthians 14:1.) The Book of Mormon describes various times in which there were many prophets. (See 1 Nephi 1:4; Words of Mormon 1:16–18.) In our day, Elder Joseph Fielding Smith declared that "all members of the Church should seek for the gift of prophecy, for their own guidance, which is the spirit by which the word of the Lord is understood and his purpose made known." (*Church History and Modern Revelation*, 3 vols. [Salt Lake City: Deseret Book Co., 1953], 1:201.)

It is important for us to understand the distinction between *a* prophet, who has the *spiritual gift of prophecy*, and *the* prophet, who has the *prophetic office*.

Some who have had the gift of prophecy have forgotten this distinction. Miriam, who is referred to as a prophetess (see Numbers 12:2), and Aaron, who was a priest, disagreed with one of the decisions of *the* prophet, Moses. The Bible describes how they "spake against Moses." (V. 1.) Moses, who the scriptures say was "meek, above all the men which were upon the face of the earth" (v. 3), may not have been able to hold his own in a debate with this rebellious priest and prophetess. But the Lord was aware of the circumstance and came into the controversy on the side of his prophet. The Bible tells us how the Lord "came down in the pillar of the cloud, and stood in the door of the tabernacle." (V. 5.) He rebuked and punished Miriam and Aaron for speaking against his prophet.

It is vital for us to honor the distinction between the prophetic *gift* and the prophetic *office*, between *a* prophet and *the* prophet.

Other gifts of the Spirit are associated with the exercise of the keys or power of the priesthood.

First, the Doctrine and Covenants says, "unto some it may be given to have all those gifts, that there may be a head, in order that every member may be profited thereby." (D&C 46:29.)

Second, we read in this same source: "And unto the bishop of the church, and unto such as God shall appoint and ordain to watch over the church and to be elders unto the church, are to have it given unto them to discern all those gifts lest there shall be any among you professing and yet be not of God." (D&C 46:27; see also 1 Corinthians 12:10.)

This power of discernment is essential if we are to distinguish between genuine spiritual gifts and the counterfeits Satan seeks to use to deceive men and women and thwart the work of God. The Prophet Joseph Smith said, "Nothing is a greater injury to the children of men than to be under the influence of a false spirit when they think they have the spirit of God." (*Teachings,* p. 205.) He also taught that "no man nor sect of men without the regular constituted authorities, the Priesthood and discerning of spirits, can tell true from false spirits." (*Teachings,* p. 213.)

Satan-inspired and man-made counterfeits of spiritual gifts have been present throughout our religious history. This is evident from the enchantments wrought by Pharaoh's sorcerers and magicians (see Exodus 7:11, 22; 8:7), and from Isaiah's warnings against "wizards that peep, and that mutter" and "them that have familiar spirits" (Isaiah 8:19). The Savior warned against false Christs and false prophets who "shall show great signs and wonders, insomuch, that, if possible, they shall deceive the very elect . . . according to the covenant." (Joseph Smith–History 1:22.) The Apostle John said, "Try the spirits whether they are of God: because many false prophets are gone out into the world." (1 John 4:1.)

Just a few months after the Church was organized, Hiram Page, one of the earliest members, was receiving revelations through a seer stone. The Lord told the Prophet Joseph Smith to tell Hiram Page privately that "those things which he has written from that stone are not of me and that Satan deceiveth him." (D&C 28:11.) The receipt of revelation had not been "appointed unto" Hiram Page, the Lord explained, "neither shall anything be appointed unto any of this church contrary to the church covenants. For all things must be done in order, and by common consent in the church, by the prayer of faith." (D&C 28:12–13.)

Here we learn that Satan gives revelations to deceive the children of men and that our protection is in following the order of the Church on who should receive revelation for what subject. In this, both men and women have equal responsibility to follow the duly ordained leaders of the Church who have the obligation to lead and, on occasion, to correct.

Early in the second year of the Church, the Lord revealed that "there are many spirits which are false spirits, which have gone forth in the earth, deceiving the world." (D&C 50:2.) The revelation on spiritual gifts tells the elders who were going forth on missions to be righteous and prayerful "that ye may not be seduced by evil spirits, or doctrines of devils, or the commandments of men; for some are of men, and others of devils." (D&C 46:7.)

Other revelations give instructions that help priesthood leaders discern the spirits and avoid being deceived. Thus, in section 52 of the Doctrine and Covenants we read that "he that speaketh, whose spirit is contrite, whose language is meek and edifieth, the same is of God if he obey mine ordinances." (V. 16.) In contrast, "he that is overcome and bringeth not forth fruits, even according to this pattern, is not of me." (V. 18.)

The Prophet's instruction that a person should not speak in tongues unless there was someone to interpret is an application of this principle. As the Lord said: "That which doth not edify is not of God, and is darkness." (D&C 50:23; see also vv. 30–35; *Teachings,* pp. 203–4.)

I have spoken of many different spiritual gifts. I have pointed out that these gifts come by the power of the Holy Ghost and that they are available to every member of the Church, male and female.

We should seek after spiritual gifts. They can lead us to God. They can shield us from the power of the adversary. They can compensate for our inadequacies and repair our imperfections. Almost a century ago President George Q. Cannon of the First Presidency taught the Saints:

"If any of us are imperfect, it is our duty to pray for the gift that will make us perfect. . . . No man ought to say, 'Oh, I cannot help this; it is my nature.' He is not justified in it, for the reason that God has promised to give strength to correct these things, and to give gifts that will eradicate them. If a man lacks wisdom, it is his duty to ask God for wisdom. The same with everything else. That is the design of God concerning His Church. He wants His Saints to be perfected in the truth. For this purpose He gives these gifts, and bestows them upon those who seek after them, in order that they may be a perfect people upon the face of the earth." (*Millennial Star,* Apr. 1894, p. 260.)

I saw that principle in action in the home in which I was raised. Having lost her husband, my widowed mother was incomplete. How she prayed for what she needed to fulfill her responsibility to raise her three small children! She was seeking, she was worthy, and she was blessed! Her prayers were answered in many ways, including the receipt of spiritual gifts. She had many, but the ones that stand out in my memory are the gifts of faith, testimony, and wisdom. She was a mighty woman in Zion, a great example of a scripture she loved to quote—Lehi's promise to his son Jacob that God "shall consecrate thine afflictions for thy gain." (2 Nephi 2:2.)

I testify to the truth of what I have taught. I testify of Jesus Christ, our Savior, whose blood has atoned for repented sins and whose resurrection has broken the bands of death for all. The gospel was restored through the Prophet Joseph Smith, whose successor, President Ezra Taft Benson, is God's prophet today.

Note

Dallin H. Oaks, "Spiritual Gifts," *Ensign,* Sept. 1986, pp. 68–72. Copyright 1986 by Corporation of the President of The Church of Jesus Christ of Latter-day Saints. Used by permission.

The Faithful Heritage of a Convert

CAROLYN J. RASMUS

ourteen years and four weeks ago this very hour, I was baptized at a stake center only four blocks from here. I could not have imagined and cannot now comprehend the life-changing effects of that act.

The first speaker on the first morning of this conference was Sister Camilla Eyring Kimball, our beloved "first lady" of the Church, a faithful sister, ninety years young and with ninety years of experience in the Church. She was followed by a panel that included the auxiliary general presidents—Dwan J. Young, Ardeth G. Kapp, and Barbara W. Winder. Two days later I am the first speaker of the morning—a convert of only fourteen years, a Mia Maid in the reckoning of Church life.

As I have focused on the difference of years of members in the Church, I began to realize that that was only one aspect of the diversity represented by the members of the Church— a diverse church made up of people with unique and different backgrounds. We represent a diversity in age, experiences, talents, family and personal situations, languages spoken and understood, education, marital status, and church callings. But more important than our diversity are the things that bind us together and unite us. For all of our diversity, we are united by our bond of faith in the Lord Jesus Christ and in our commitment to The Church of Jesus Christ of Latter-day Saints. We are people of faith. It is the thing which sets us apart from the world. It is what makes us brothers and sisters in the fullest

Carolyn J. Rasmus is the administrative assistant to the Young Women General Presidency and has held numerous callings in ward and stake Young Women organizations. She received an Ed.D. in physical education with minors in child development and learning disabilities from Brigham Young University, where she is also professor of physical education–sports. Sister Rasmus was the executive assistant to the president of BYU and was also chair of the faculty advisory council for a time.

sense of the word. Faith is the unifying factor that created a common bond between me and Sister Kimball, and Sisters Young, Kapp, and Winder. It is what unites us with people around the world, with our next door neighbors or with the person seated beside or behind or in front of you. We are sisters and brothers of a common faith. It is our faith, I believe, that not only brings us together but which will in the end be the only thing that really matters.

I began preparing for my talk by going to two of my favorite sources: the scriptures and the *Oxford English Dictionary*. What I have come to share today is not a neatly wrapped package but ideas that have come to me as I've thought and read and struggled with the title, "The Faithful Heritage of a Convert." These are offerings, given in the hope that they might trigger your own thoughts and ideas that will have personal meaning.

The dictionary tells us that *heritage* is something transmitted by or acquired from a predecessor. At that first conference session our hearts and spirits were touched as our faithful leader sisters shared with us that kind of a heritage as they related faith-promoting stories of their pioneer ancestors. I have no such direct heritage. Many others of you do not either, for now nearly half the total adult membership of the Church is composed of first-generation members.

But in an eternal sense, we all share a common heritage, which extends far beyond the days of handcarts and covered wagons. The scriptures tell us of our more important and common heritage, a heritage which comes from the fact that we are all sisters and brothers whose heavenly parents love us—we are literal offspring of God. George Q. Cannon tells us that as His children "there is not an attribute we ascribe to Him that we do not possess, though they may be dormant or in embryo." (George Q. Cannon, *Gospel Truth* [Salt Lake City: Deseret Book, 1974], 1:1.) We are also taught of our infinite worth and are told we have a divine and individual mission.

In the process of my conversion, knowledge of this heritage was reawakened in me. My spirit responded to what I believe I had known long ago when you and I were together in the presence of Heavenly Father. In addition to that eternal heri-

41

tage, I—like many of you—inherited some other things in the process of conversion: among those things I include new scriptures and new knowledge and insights.

This triple combination, with my name imprinted on the cover, was given to me on the last day of class by a group of students who inscribed this message:

"Dear Miss Rasmus,

"You have shared with us things that are important and close to you. In return, we would like to give you something that means a great deal to us. And, we want you to know that we give it to you with a lot of love and respect.

"Sincerely,

"Your fans,

"BYU Summer School, Second Session, 1970."

It was to become a gift that made a difference. I was touched that a group of students cared enough about me that they wanted to give me a gift, though I could not begin to comprehend what it was they had really shared.

It is more difficult to identify specific new knowledge or insights gained as a result of the conversion process. Much of what I learned and am learning is, I believe, a literal reawakening of things known before, knowledge brought to this life from another. After I'd been at BYU for more than a year, several women who lived in Provo arranged an all-day hiking expedition on a beautiful fall day in October. I was eager to leave my studies and head for the mountains.

But as it neared 10:00 A.M. they began looking for a comfortable place to sit down. I didn't have any idea it was general conference. I didn't even know what general conference was. I certainly didn't know my fellow hikers were equipped with a transistor radio. I was without question a captive audience, and although I said nothing to any of the hiking group, when I returned home that evening I wrote on my daily calendar, "Everything sounds so right." It was, I believe now, a time of reawakening to truths learned long ago in a very different setting.

One of the things I became conscious of early was the reality of the still, small voice—a power that communicated to

42

me thoughts and ideas I could not conceive in my finite mind. These stories illustrate what I mean. I made the decision to go to BYU because of my professional acquaintance with Dr. Leona Holbrook. We were kindred spirits from the moment we met and, quite frankly, I would have gone to study wherever she taught. When I first told her of my interest in enrolling at BYU, she suggested I visit the campus before making a final decision. She knew of my smoking habit and that I dearly loved wine. (I used to have a friend bring my favorite vintage by the case from her home in Minnesota.) Leona merely said to me, "BYU is a unique place. Visit before you make your decision." And so more than a year before I became a student, I visited BYU and recorded this after a two-day visit: "My stop at BYU only served to convince me that I made the right decision. Having been there made me realize I'll even be able to give up my much-loved wine for what I'll receive in return."

Other experiences followed that helped me become increasingly aware of what I now know was the light of Christ. Having decided to fast for the first time in my life, I was unsettled and unable to concentrate on studying for a statistics test. Finally, I knelt down to pray. I have no recollection of the prayer, but these thoughts came into my mind, and I felt impressed to record them. On a scrap piece of paper I wrote:

"October 12, 1970, 8:45 A.M. Go now, my child, for there is much work to be done. I send my Spirit to be with you to enable you to work and think clearly, to accomplish all that lies before you this day. Go and know that I am with you in all things, and later return to me, coming to me with real intent of prayer. Know that I am the Lord, that all things are possible to them who call upon my name. Take comfort in these words. Fill your heart with joy and gladness, not sorrow and despair. Lo, I am with you always, even unto the end of the world. Know me as Comforter and Savior."

I also had the impression, months before my baptism, that I should begin paying tithing. As members, we all know about the gray envelopes imprinted with the bishop's name. But, what do you do with tithing monies if you don't know the procedure? Each paycheck for three months, I took 10 percent of my meager student wages and put the cash in a white envelope, which I carefully hid in my underwear drawer. When Bishop Mayfield interviewed me relative to my worthiness to be baptized, I proudly produced evidence of my belief in the law of tithing.

Only two weeks before I joined the Church I sat in a sacrament meeting. As I passed the tray of bread from the person on one side of me to the other, these words came pounding into my head: "How much longer can you pass by the bread of life? Know, believe, do. Know that Joseph Smith was a prophet and that through him my church has been restored in these latter days. Know and believe, then do . . . be baptized into my church." Such thoughts are unsettling to say the least. I thought, and continue to think, about those words — "know, believe, do."

There is much knowledge in the world — both secular and spiritual. We are told of the importance of gaining knowledge, but that is only the first step. During this women's conference Sister Naomi Randall, author of the words to "I Am a Child of God," told us about President Kimball's contribution to the lyrics of that familiar song. He asked her to change the word *know* to *do* — "teach me all that I must *do* to live with him someday."

Her story triggered my thoughts back to the time those words came into my mind — "know, believe, do" — and I came to a new insight. In preparation for this women's conference, I read the book *The Teachings of Spencer W. Kimball,* a compilation of excerpts from President Kimball's many talks and addresses. (Salt Lake City: Bookcraft, 1982.) In the section on faith, he makes repeated reference to one scripture. "If any man will *do* [the Father's] will he shall *know* of the doctrine, whether it be of God, or whether I speak of myself." (John 7:17; italics added.)

Initially, my interest in the Church came as a result of what I observed in the lives of others — how people interacted with each other and how they treated me. Quite frankly, I was not interested in what people knew. If anyone had asked me, "Do you want to know more?" I would have answered, "No." But I could not ignore what I saw people doing.

I will never forget going (I think "being taken" is probably more correct) to the ground-breaking service for the Provo Temple. It occurred less than a month after my arrival in Provo. I did not know the significance of that event, but what I saw and felt touched me deeply. I listened intently as a father quietly and patiently responded to the incessant questioning of his young family. He was kind and gentle as he held them and talked with them. And then that hillside of people began singing "The Spirit of God Like a Fire Is Burning." They all knew all the words without a hymnbook, and I felt the Spirit of God.

A woman I remember meeting only once left a homemade pie and a note on our doorstep. She wanted to welcome my mother who was coming to visit from Ohio. I knew nothing at that time about visiting teachers or that she was mine. But I remember well my feelings that she had done this for me, that she knew who I was and that she cared enough about me to take time to do something special.

Only after my baptism would I know that the Kocherhans family always made it a point to sit near me every sacrament meeting. "Because," said the father of the family and the priest-hood bearer who baptized me, "we wanted you to feel our spirit and of our love for you." And, oh, how I did. I was not anxious to "know of the doctrine," but I could not ignore what people were doing. Likewise, I later became aware that many ward members had fasted and prayed in my behalf.

It is interesting to me that the first book of the New Testament, after the four gospels, is entitled "The Acts of the Apostles." It is not the "lectures" or "sermons" of the Apostles, but the "acts." In the process of studying what the apostles did, we learn the doctrine—we come to know what they believed and why they did what they did.

We can read about how to ride a bicycle. We might even be able to explain it to others, but we really only know how to ride a bicycle after we have actually done it. I do not want to have surgery performed by physicians who know only what is written in the textbook. I want to make sure they have actually performed the surgery. Then I will believe they know what they are about.

And so it was with me. I am convinced that one of the major, and certainly the initial, factors in my conversion came as a result of what I saw people doing—their actions were evidence for me that they knew something I wanted to learn more about.

But John 7:17 tells us that we can *know* the doctrine if we will *do* His will. I believe I came to know the law of tithing by paying tithing—by doing it. The knowledge that scripture study and prayer and fasting can bring understanding and insight came to have meaning to me only after I did them.

We are inheritors of a gospel that is action oriented. There is nothing passive about phrases like "awake and arouse your faculties," "experiment upon my words," "exercise a particle of faith," or words such as "desired, pondered, believed." (Alma 32:27; 1 Nephi 11:1.) This is a gospel of action, of doing. No wonder President Kimball had as his motto, "DO IT."

In a First Presidency Message in 1975, President Kimball encouraged us to "read and understand and apply [or do] the principles and inspired counsel found in the [scriptures]." He promised us that if we did so, "we shall discover that our personal *acts* of righteousness will also bring *personal revelation* or *inspiration* . . . into our own lives." (*Ensign*, Sept. 1975, p. 4; italics in original.) It is he who also reminded us that "if [we] will do [God's] will, [we] shall know of the doctrine." (John 7:17.)

Sometimes we know something but do nothing about it. In fact, there is often a discrepancy between what we say we know and what we do. I am convinced, from personal experience, that it is this discrepancy that creates inner strife and turmoil—a literal wrenching of our souls. Oh, that we might learn to act with integrity, having the moral courage to make our actions (our doing) consistent with our knowledge of right and wrong, to be able to say with Job, "Till I die I will not remove mine integrity from me." (Job 27:5.)

I had another thought as I read the dictionary definition of *heritage*. It said, "Heritage may imply anything passed on to heirs or succeeding generations." I had always thought of heritage from the perspective of what I might receive from others. As I read that definition, I began to think about what I could pass on to others. We sometimes forget that our heritage is being created by us right now. Granted, we can build upon the past, but our heritage, that which we will someday give to others, is in process now—we are literally creating our heritage, whether we are twelve or eighteen, forty or eighty.

I began thinking about what I would pass on, what I would leave for others that might be meaningful—something others might build upon. I don't have a magic list. I don't think my list is even complete, but on this thirtieth day of March, 1985, I want to leave as a heritage to others four things: a message of hope and optimism, my commitment to The Church of Jesus Christ of Latter-day Saints, my faith in Jesus Christ as our Savior, and my belief in the principles of the restored gospel.

First, a message of hope and optimism. If we read only the daily news of the world, we would have our attention focused on crime, immorality, dishonesty, corruption, and abuse of every kind. If we focused only on the social ills of our day, we would be overcome with feelings of gloom and despair. But we know so much more. This is a glorious gospel and we, of all people, have cause to rejoice, for we have been given the knowledge to be able to view things in an eternal perspective. Without such perspective, it would be easy to lose our way in what Elder Maxwell calls this "secular dispensation of despair." (Neal A. Maxwell, *The Smallest Part* [Salt Lake City: Deseret Book, 1973], p. 16.) Elder Maxwell calls our attention to the young servant of Elisha who feared for the future until the Lord opened his eyes so that he could see what Elisha saw.

"And when the servant of the man of God was risen early, and gone forth, behold, an host compassed the city both with horses and chariots. And his servant said unto him, Alas, my master! how shall we do?

"And he answered, Fear not: for they that be with us are more than they that be with them.

"And Elisha prayed, and said, Lord, I pray thee, open his eyes, that he may see. And the Lord opened the eyes of the young man; and he saw: and, behold, the mountain was full of horses and chariots of fire round about Elisha." (2 Kings 6:15–17.)

When we are feeling overwhelmed and we doubt that as individuals we could ever make any difference, we need to be reminded of Elisha and of the fact that we are not alone. We are told that we are agents, on the Lord's errand; to "be not weary in well-doing, for [we] are laying the foundation of a great work. And out of small things proceedeth that which is great." (D&C 64:33.) We learn from modern-day scripture that the Lord has "given the heavenly hosts and . . . angels charge concerning [us]." (D&C 84:42.)

I also hope to share with others my commitment to building and defending the kingdom of God. I believe we learn what commitment is really about in the holy temple of God. We come to understand what it means to obey and sacrifice and consecrate our time and talents. In this day and in this land we are not presently called upon to make physical sacrifices — we are not driven from our homes, we have not been called to pull handcarts or to leave our homes and establish new communities. But ultimately to understand the principle of commitment, our knowledge of this principle will, like all others, need to be translated into action. In 1970, President Harold B. Lee said:

"We have some tight places to go before the Lord is through with this Church and the world in this dispensation. The gospel was restored to prepare a people ready to receive Him. You may not like what comes from the authority of the Church. It may contradict your social views, it may interfere with some of your social life, but if you listen to these things as if from the mouth of the Lord Himself with patience and faith, the promise is, 'the gates of Hell shall not prevail against you; yea, and the Lord God will disperse the powers of darkness from before you, and cause the heavens to shake for your good and his name's glory.' (D&C 21:6.)" ("Uphold the Hands of the President of the Church," *Improvement Era*, Dec. 1970, p. 126.) I believe we will be "tossed to and fro, and carried about with every wind of doctrine" (Ephesians 4:14) unless we are covenanted and committed before we are confronted with difficult choices and hard times.

I want to commit to trying to live in such a way that others might know by what I do that when I raise my arm to the square to sustain the General Authorities and officers of The Church of Jesus Christ of Latter-day Saints, I am anxious and ready to respond to their counsel and direction.

I want to commit to trying to live with my eye and mind single to his glory and purposes. (See D&C 88:67–68.) I find it easy to commit to such a thing in the quiet and solitude and aloneness of my room, but I want to learn to be able to have such focus in busy and rushed and difficult situations.

Finally, I leave for you and others a testimony of my faith in the Lord Jesus Christ. When we are feeling discouraged or put upon, left out or neglected, overwhelmed, unloved, ignored, or sorely tempted, we need to have brought to our minds that He "suffer[ed] pains and afflictions and temptations of every kind; and this that the word might be fulfilled which saith he will take upon him the pains and the sicknesses of his people.... that he may know according to the flesh how to succor his people according to their infirmities." (Alma 7:11–12.)

I believe we will come to know that truth as we try, as His agents and a covenanted people, to "bear one another's burdens . . . and are willing to mourn with those that mourn . . . and comfort those that stand in need of comfort" (Mosiah 18:8–9), as we strive to "lift up the hands which hang down, and strengthen the feeble knees." (D&C 81:5.) I believe with President Kimball that "God does notice us, and he watches over us. But it is usually through another person that he meets our needs." ("Small Acts of Service," *Ensign,* Dec. 1974, p. 5.)

I would leave my testimony of the boy prophet Joseph Smith and especially of the process that led to that great theophany. The boy had identified the problem (there were many sects and denominations), and he had searched the scriptures. Then he went to the Lord in humble prayer to inquire of Him. (Which church should I join?) And he modeled for us the attribute of patience as he spent the next ten years waiting and studying and preparing—all of which were necessary before the Church could be established and the work go forward.

I have great faith in the literal promises of Him who is our exemplar of the perfect life. But lest we become discouraged in the pursuit of perfection, we should take comfort in President Kimball's encouragement that "working toward perfection is not a one-time decision, but a process to be pursued throughout one's lifetime." (*Ensign,* Nov. 1978, p. 6.) In my own life I find I make periodic progress forward and then slip back into old habits and doubts. Sometimes I'm not pleased with what I do when compared with what I know. It takes courage to see ourselves as less than perfect.

Finally, I have faith that our Heavenly Father wants us to return to Him. We agreed to come here so that we might be tried and tested and proven, but we came here with the full expectation that we could succeed, and with the help of the Savior we would, if we endured to the end.

> And someday, when he's proven me,
> I'll see him face to face,
> But just for here and now I walk by faith.

(Janice Kapp Perry, "I Walk by Faith," 1985.)

COPING WITH HARD REALITIES

We each deal with these difficult aspects of mortality in individual and unique ways that involve choice and accountability.

—DEANNE FRANCIS

A Latter-day Saint Theology of Suffering

FRANCINE R. BENNION

*I*t is not my purpose here to give careful definition of the term *suffering* or to distinguish between various kinds of suffering. For purposes of this discussion, *suffering* is anything that hurts badly, in any way.

Nor is it my purpose to answer all questions about suffering, or even to suggest that we all have the same questions. We have our own quests, and the search for peace must be our own. My intent is to discuss the reservoir to which many of us go for understanding and comfort in time of anguish.

My friend Sheila Brown came out of brain surgery with one side of her body paralyzed and with her speech and sight badly impaired. As we worked one day at stretching and relaxing her muscles, Sheila asked me what I was going to talk about at the BYU Women's Conference.

"A Latter-day Saint theology of suffering."

"Oh," she said, searching for words and trying to form them, "I think — you should talk about theology of — courage — hope — like looking out a window."

"I think it's the same thing," I replied.

We are accustomed to talking of fragments of theology — a topic here, an assumption or tradition there, often out of context with the whole. We are a people accustomed also to fragments of scripture out of context — a phrase here, a verse there, words that say something appropriate to the matter at hand, and ring with clarity and conviction. We have to do it: we haven't time or ability to say everything at once. Sometimes,

Francine R. Bennion received a B.A. from Brigham Young University and an M.A. from Ohio State University and has taught English part time at both institutions. Her extensive Church service has included membership on the Relief Society and Young Women general boards, president of the BYU Eleventh Stake Relief Society, ward organist, and teacher in the auxiliaries.

however, the clarity becomes blurred and the conviction open to question when a person puts some fragments with others. For example, what do you make of the following?

2 Nephi 2:25	"Men are, that they might have joy."
Job 5:7	"Man is born unto trouble, as the sparks fly upward."

Deuteronomy 4:29–31	"But if from thence thou shalt seek the Lord thy God, thou shalt find him, if thou seek him with all thy heart and with all thy soul.
	"When thou art in tribulation, and all these things are come upon thee, even in the latter days, if thou turn to the Lord thy God, and shalt be obedient unto his voice;
	" . . . he will not forsake thee. . . ."
Psalm 22:1–2	"My God, my God, why hast thou forsaken me? why art thou so far from helping me, and from the words of my roaring?
	"O my God, I cry in the daytime, but thou hearest not; and in the night season, and am not silent."
Matthew 27:46	"My God, my God, why hast thou forsaken me?"

Abraham 3:18	"Spirits . . . have no beginning; they existed before, they shall have no end, they shall exist after, for they are gnolaum, or eternal."
2 Nephi 2:14	"God . . . hath created all things, both the heavens and the earth, and all things that in them are, both things to act and things to be acted upon."

Proverbs 3:13   "Happy is the man that findeth wisdom, and the man that getteth understanding."

Ecclesiastes 1:18   "In much wisdom is much grief: and he that increaseth knowledge increaseth sorrow."

One function of theology is to provide a comprehensive framework that gives meaning to the fragments and the seeming contradictions or paradoxes which they suggest. Theology provides a framework that binds diversity and complexity into a more simple net with which we can make some sense even of things we don't fully understand.

If we live long enough, we find diverse views and contrasting fragments not only in scripture but also in life. For example, Dorothy Bramhall went to Hawaii in February for the birth of a grandchild. She went also for a visit with a longtime friend, not LDS, who had lost two sons in a traffic accident and then struggled with her own cancer and amputations for many years. Dorothy wrote:

"It's been a week of varied emotions. My friend, Jean Kerr, died the morning after I arrived. It seems I'm destined to spend part of my beach time in Hawaii contemplating the death of a good friend. The beach, at least for me, like the mountains, is a good place for such contemplation. Again, my thoughts have been drawn to the 'why' of it all. For those of us in the Church, there are at least a few answers to that question. But as I look at my friend and wonder what her purpose in life was—it seems that suffering has been the *only* purpose.... Suffering without a sense of purpose seems bitter indeed. Her mother said her husband prayed all night for her to die. Does one who doesn't believe pray to anyone or anything? Or is it merely another way of saying—he yearned for or hoped that she would die? Do you think such a prayer will be heard when all those given for her healing have not been?

"Enough! My grandson was born at 5 A.M. Sat. Eight lbs., 8 ozs.! I don't know where she put him—from the back you would never know she was pregnant. He has lots of black hair, and I'm hoping maybe this one will be brown eyed. This is a miracle baby. When he was born the doctor showed them that the cord was knotted. The reason the baby survived is that his cord was unusually long, and the knot was never pulled tight. They are feeling very blessed. It's always such a humbling feeling to look at a newborn—such utter perfection! I can hardly wait to hold him."[1]

The same week, the daughter of another of my friends gave birth to a premature Down's syndrome child who has already had two of the six operations needed for survival. On March 2, a report released by the World Bank estimated that 730 million people in poor countries, not including China, lacked the income in 1980 to buy enough food to give them the energy for an active working life.

One function of any religion is to explain such a world as this, to provide a theology that makes sense of love and joy and miracles but also of suffering and struggle and lack of miracles. Good theology makes sense of what is possible but also of what is presently real and probable. In this twentieth century, it is not enough that a theology of suffering explain *my* experience; it must also explain the child lying in a gutter in India, the woman crawling across the Ethiopian desert to find a weed to eat, and the fighting and misery of many humans because of pride, greed, or fear in a powerful few. Satisfying theology must explain the child sexually abused or scarred for life, or the astronaut who is blown up and leaves a family motherless or fatherless. Good theology of suffering explains *all* human suffering, not just the suffering of those who feel they know God's word and are His chosen people.

It is not enough that theology be *either* rational *or* faith promoting. It must be both. It is not enough that satisfying theology be mastered by a few expert scholars, teachers, and leaders. It must be comfortably carried by ordinary people. It is not enough that theology help me to understand God. It must also help me to understand myself and my world.

Theology does not prevent all hurt and anguish. No knowledge of theology can remove all pain, weakness, or nausea from all terminal cancer. Nor can it fill an empty stomach. What sound theology *can* do is to help those who believe it to make some sense of the suffering, of themselves, and of God, such sense that they can proceed with a measure of hope, courage, compassion, and understanding of themselves even in anguish.

There is no single theology of suffering in our church, one framework uniform in all respects in the minds of all leaders and all other members. Though we may share the same scripture, the same revelation, prophets, and belief that God and Christ are real, we have various frameworks for putting them together and for seeing suffering, either our own or someone else's. One person thinks God sends suffering to teach us or to test us. Another thinks God or Satan can affect only our response to the suffering, and some think it is Satan who is causing the suffering. Others think there should be no suffering at all if we are righteous and certainly no misunderstanding at all about why it is happening. These are only a few of the varieties of LDS belief about the origins of suffering, and however contradictory they be, each can be supported by fragments of scripture.[2]

We do not use identical principles or patterns to bind together fragments of scripture and life. In this twentieth century, with the history of the world before us, each of us has taken ideas and patterns from various sources to form our personal theologies of suffering. The complexity and power of those sources are evident in the story of Jephthah.

According to the book of Judges, chapter 11, Jephthah was asked to lead Israel against invading Ammonites.

"And Jephthah said unto the elders of Gilead, If . . . the Lord deliver them before me, shall I be your head?

"And the elders of Gilead said unto Jephthah, The Lord be witness between us, if we do not so according to thy words.

"Then Jephthah went with the elders of Gilead, and the people made him head and captain over them. . . .

"Then the Spirit of the Lord came upon Jephthah. . . .

"And Jephthah vowed a vow unto the Lord, and said, If thou shalt without fail deliver the children of Ammon into mine hands,

"Then it shall be, that whatsoever cometh forth of the doors of my house to meet me, when I return in peace from the children of Ammon, shall surely be the Lord's, and I will offer it up for a burnt offering.

"So Jephthah passed over unto the children of Ammon to fight against them; and the Lord delivered them into his hands.

"And he smote them . . . with a very great slaughter. Thus the children of Ammon were subdued before the children of Israel.

"And Jephthah came to Mizpeh unto his house, and, behold, his daughter came out to meet him with timbrels and with dances: and she was his only child; beside her he had neither son nor daughter.

"And it came to pass, when he saw her, that he rent his clothes, and said, Alas, my daughter! thou hast brought me very low, and thou art one of them that trouble me: for I have opened my mouth unto the Lord, and I cannot go back.

"And she said unto him, My father, if thou hast opened thy mouth unto the Lord, do to me according to that which hath proceeded out of thy mouth; forasmuch as the Lord hath taken vengeance for thee of thine enemies, even of the children of Ammon.

"And she said unto her father, Let this thing be done for me: let me alone two months, that I may go up and down upon the mountains, and bewail my virginity, I and my fellows.

"And he said, Go. And he sent her away for two months: and she went with her companions, and bewailed her virginity upon the mountains.

"And it came to pass at the end of two months, that she returned unto her father, who did with her according to his vow which he had vowed." (Judges 11:9–11; 29–39.)

As the story is told, Jephthah makes the sacrifice because he believes it to be right. At the core of his and his daughter's theology are these principles: God controls human events and determines either victory or defeat in battle. God can be bargained with. God gives Israel victory *because* of Jephthah's all-encompassing vow, his willingness to give God anything he has. God's law requires that the vow be kept. According to our record in the book of Numbers, "If a man vow a vow unto the Lord, or swear an oath to bind his soul with a bond; he shall not break his word, he shall do according to all that proceedeth out of his mouth." (Numbers 30:2.)

A human being's function is to obey the law. If God had wanted the obedient daughter saved, He could have prevented her from dancing out at so inopportune a moment.

We do not all read the same things into Jephthah's story, or into sacrifice.[3] Even in so short a story, the context for suffering is complex and today provokes questions such as these: Who is really responsible for the suffering in this story? Jephthah? God? The religious leaders who taught the theology that contributed to the making and keeping of the vow? Persons who developed a social system in which a daughter is her father's property? What of Jephthah's wife, who isn't even mentioned? What about Jephthah's father and harlot mother, and the half-brothers who threw Jephthah out of the house earlier in his life and perhaps contributed to his great desire for the power that victory would bring? (Judges 11:1–3.) What about Jacob, who set a precedent by bargaining with God? (Genesis 28:20.) Or Moses, who, without regard to circumstances, seemed to teach that keeping a vow was more important than "selfish" compassion?

This list does not, of course, exhaust the questions, which go beyond reasons for Jephthah's vow; for example, is obedience always a virtue? Is the major difference between God and Satan just a matter of who's in charge, demanding obedience?

Custom can make the whole matter of Jephthah's vow seem simple, and we tend to like simplicity and clarity, even if it means ignoring some things. There is power in simplicity. Some thousand and more years after the time of the judges, Paul the apostle praised Jephthah for his faith without condemning him for ambition or rashness. (Hebrews 11:32–34.)

Today, many who do think Jephthah rash nevertheless have "simply" made his version of God their own: a God who controls all human events; a God who can and must be bargained with; a God who considers unquestioning obedience to be the highest good—not just the *means* to goodness, but goodness itself; a God who causes suffering in the innocent and also authorizes theology that fosters it. Many who believe in such a God either ignore or are confused by inconsistency with other scriptures that seem to speak of God's valuing agency above obedience (e.g., Moses 4:1–3), love above tradition (e.g., Matthew 5), and the human heart above ritual sacrifice (e.g., Isaiah 1:11–17).

What do *you* think about Jephthah, his vow, and his God? Your answer will depend in part upon your own version of theology.

Does it really matter what we think? Can't we just be kind and patient, without worrying about various points of theology?

It matters. For one thing, our assumptions affect how kind and patient we are likely to become. What Jephthah *believed* was central to what he did about suffering, and what we *believe* is central to what we do about it. For example, if we believe that inflicting suffering will further God's work or glory, we may inflict it, as Irish and Lebanese and Iranians are currently doing, or as a father did by punishing his young son by putting his hands under scalding water, which nearly destroyed them, or as a husband is doing by telling his wife she can do nothing unless he tells her she can.

If we believe God wants suffering, we may not take responsible action to relieve or prevent it. Thirty-five years ago, one of my schoolteachers would not take medical help for a lump in her thigh because "God had given it to her." In Relief Society one Sunday last year, a class member told us we shouldn't concern ourselves with events in the newspaper because God is planning destruction before the Millennium anyway, and all we should concern ourselves with is our own righteousness and that of our children, and then we'll be all right. A few years ago, one young woman's confusion about God and suffering was central to her anguish and paralysis in the face of repeated violence: "I don't know what it is God's trying to teach me with my husband's temper."

Many who believe God is causing the suffering will not. or feel they cannot, ask Him for help or comfort at the very time they need it most.

Another of the reasons our theology of suffering matters is that we may live comfortably with a framework which has inherent holes and contradictions as long as the suffering is someone else's or as long as our own suffering isn't very great. But holes and contradictions have a way of becoming very important when anguish is our own or when we feel the pain of persons we care about. Job's friends said to him:

"Behold, thou hast instructed many, and thou hast strengthened the weak hands.

"Thy words have upholden him that was falling, and thou hast strengthened the feeble knees.

"But now it is come upon thee, and thou faintest; it toucheth thee, and thou art troubled." (Job 4:3–5.)

If, like Job, we find that the comforts we've offered others aren't sufficient for our own experience, then the suffering itself, however great, is not the only problem. The problem is also that the universe and our ability to make sense of it have fallen apart, and we are without hope or trust in ourselves or in God.

Theology can become an even heavier problem than the anguish of suffering itself. If we believe suffering shouldn't exist, but it does; or suffering is God's way of testing and teaching, but what can a wailing infant be proving or learning; or prayer should cure the problem, but it hasn't—then it is not only the suffering that troubles us but also the great cracks in a universe that should make sense but doesn't. I have seen the pain of persons in this place, the pain of persons fumbling with their long-held assumptions when the ancient questions rise afresh, though they had thought them already answered: Why is this happening? Can I stand it? What can I do? What am I? Is God real, or powerful, or good? What is life for? What does He want us to do with it?

Important to one's struggles with such questions are the implications of elements at the core of one's theology—for example, Latter-day Saint belief that we can become more like God, our Eternal Father, not just obey Him or imitate Him or follow His Son, though these things are part of the process, but become gods ourselves with His help.

61

For many Christians, such doctrine is scandalous, radical, heretical. On February 17, 1600, the Dominican priest Bruno of Nola was burned at the stake as a heretic. Among other things, he had taught that there is an infinity of worlds, the universe is eternal, and "from a more vile creature I become a God."[4] Today there is widespread agreement that there is indeed an infinity of worlds, and that so-called matter or energy is eternal, though fluctuating in form and state. But the idea of humans becoming gods is still considered by traditional Christians to be a vain, presumptuous, heretical notion.[5]

Even among those who believe it, the idea of our possible state as gods sometimes remains as nebulous as traditional views of pink clouds and golden harps. A group of BYU Honors students was discussing Voltaire and "the best of all possible worlds."

"Tell me," I said, "what you consider to be the best of all possible worlds."

"It would be like the celestial kingdom."

"What is that like?"

"Well, there won't be problems like we have here."

"What kind of problems?"

"Well, for one thing, everyone will be — happy. There won't be any unkindness. No one there will be rejected or abused, or laughed at, or ignored."

"Oh," I said. "Are you suggesting that God experiences none of these things now?"

And then there was silence, for a moment.

In wanting to get to the celestial kingdom, these students had more awareness of traditional struggle-free utopias than of our own God and our own world. The celestial kingdom was a place to get away from suffering, not a place to understand it and address it in ways consistent with joy and love and agency.

It is not only professed points of doctrine such as potential godhood or the celestial kingdom that matter but also the meaning and larger framework that a person gives to them. The larger framework gives meaning to the fragments. I haven't heard anyone in or out of our church ask why God caused seven persons to fall in bits to the bottom of the sea when the space shuttle *Challenger* exploded. We are accustomed to a methodical framework for space travel, and we looked within that framework for explanations of the disaster. A commission began to examine video reruns, O-rings, materials, workmanship, memos, organization, and decision making, among other things, to identify and address problems before proceeding with the next manned space project. The process was complex, but even minor steps had been recorded, and a meticulous report was possible.

We can make such a report to trace the steps in many kinds of suffering, but usually we have neither time nor ability to reduce all causes and all effects to a satisfying xeroxed page.[6] Even when we can do it quite accurately, we are most likely reporting *how* the suffering came about, not *why*. Some twenty years ago, a man watched his mother die miserably of cancer and then, closing up the house, said, "I cannot pray to a God who would let my little mother suffer like that." He did not want a step-by-step report on how cancer causes pain, or how she got the cancer. He wanted to know why cancer exists at all, why there is pain, why God doesn't prevent it, why the innocent suffer, why a small frail human would have such undeserved hurt. What purpose could justify such anguish? What comprehensive model of existence could make sense of it?

We have not the mind of God. We see through a glass darkly now and will till we meet Him and ourselves face to face and "know as we are known."[7] There are times we must say, "I don't know." If we think we know everything, it is a sure sign we do not. But we are capable of learning much about this world and of considering what difference LDS doctrines can make to how we put together our experience, our diverse scriptures, our traditions, and well-supported but contradictory theological explanations. The better we understand what *is* at the core of LDS doctrine, the better we can distinguish what is *not*. We need not shroud ourselves helplessly in a crazy quilt stitched haphazardly from Old Testament theology, such as that of Jephthah, with a few patches of utopian thought and LDS doctrine embroidered on top. We can extend our understanding of LDS principles and use them as the core for a framework with which to make some sense of contradictory fragments.

Of course it may seem simpler to stay on well-worn traditional ground, but God—and this is one of the most important things we believe about Him—has invited us to go further, to make suffering worth the trouble and to meet it as well as we can. We can be in the process of learning to do that whatever our current limitations or circumstances. Though our search for understanding be long or incomplete, it can lead us to courage, peace, and an increasingly truer sense of ourselves and God.

The traditional views are that we are alive because God put us here, or because Eve and Adam fell from innocence and trouble-free paradise through disobedience. These views are expressed in scripture. The Latter-day Saints believe, however, that these traditional views are fragmentary because they leave out several important things—for example, that we have existed without beginning and that we are here because we chose to come.[8] We are here not just because God decided it would be a good idea and made it happen, not just because Adam and Eve fell and we automatically followed, but because *we chose to come.* However essential what God or Eve or Adam did to make it possible, we believe the decision to be born was our own. Our very brief accounts of life before this earth suggest that we chose as Eve chose, and we defended that choice in whatever kind of war can take place among spirits.[9] Our birth is evidence of courage and faith, not helplessness, shame, and disobedience, and yet we must make sense of conflicting reports about it, seemingly contradictory fragments about it. If we are to make sense of them, we had better understand well the implications of those brief fragments we have about our existence before human life began.

We don't know if there were several possibilities of which we have no record, but I doubt there was a never-never land where we could have been happy children without responsibility forever. Apparently there was a point at which we had to grow up or choose not to. Our scriptures suggest that there

were unavoidable decisions to be made consciously and re-
sponsibly by all inhabitants in the premortal council, as in
Eden. We could not be mere observers, only thinking about
the decision, only imagining what might happen if we made
it, only talking about the meaning of it all. At any rate, God's
directive to Alma when he watched good women and children
being burned alive in Ammonihah suggests that it was not
enough to imagine what might have happened if they were
burned to death, or what might have become of the persons
who were doing it. (See Alma 14:11 in context.) God didn't
want to know just what *could* happen and neither, apparently,
did they in the beginning.

At any rate, we are told that there were two alternatives.
Lucifer proposed a way so different from God's that it would
have destroyed this universe in which God speaks of *I* and
thou, *they* and *we*, this universe in which Elohim and Jehovah
speak of their own names and also address *by name* Eve,
Joseph, Moses, Mary, Abraham, Helaman, Peter, and Emma.
Lucifer would have for all of us only one name, one will, one
identity: his own. It was not obedience and "success" (by his
definition) he would prevent; rather it was disobedience and
failure he would not allow. In his universe, no one would be
hurt or afraid. He would allow only whatever experience and
identity he chose for us, and if we met pleasure, pain, or success,
it would be wholly because of himself, not because of ourselves.
The wonder is that Lucifer's intended universe is exactly the
universe many now attribute to God, or want from Him.

God offered a profoundly different possibility, that with
His help we meet and create reality as individuals in a universe
of law and personal agency, and ultimately choose who we
want to be, choosing to become more like Himself if that is
what we want, choosing to become gods if that is what we
truly want for all eternity.[10] Law in God's universe is a matter
of processes or relationships that are knowable and predict-
able, not whimsical or inconsistent. Such law is inherent in all
matters. Agency in such a universe is not only the capacity for
moral choice, but more largely, the capacity for real thought,
action, and invention, with inherent consequences for oneself

and others. An agent is one whose self cannot be permanently determined by other persons, or by events and circumstances. The implications of this doctrine are important to our suffering whether we live in England or Africa, with or without current understanding of God's ways.

We wanted life, however high the cost. We suffer because we were willing to pay the cost of *being* and of being here with others in their ignorance and inexperience as well as our own. We suffer because we are willing to pay the costs of living with laws of nature, which operate quite consistently whether or not we understand them or can manage them. We suffer because, like Christ in the desert, we apparently did not say we would come only if God would change all our stones to bread in time of hunger. We were willing to *know* hunger. Like Christ in the desert, we did not ask God to let us try falling or being bruised only on condition that He catch us before we touch ground and save us from real hurt. We were willing to *know* hurt. Like Christ, we did not agree to come only if God would make everyone bow to us and respect us, or admire us and understand us. Like Christ, we came to be ourselves, addressing and creating reality. We are finding out who we are and who we can become regardless of immediate environment or circumstances.

What is the point of that? What is the point of knowing reality and being ourselves, of suffering as Dorothy's friend Jean Kerr suffered and as many other people suffer daily? Why did this matter so much?

One reason we were willing to pay the high costs of continuing to address reality and become ourselves is that God told us we can become more like Himself. We can become more abundantly alive, with ultimate fulness of truth, joy, and love — fulness impossible for souls unable to take real part in creating it, souls ignorant of good or evil, pleasure or pain, souls afraid of the unknown.

According to my understanding of scripture, we are not preparing now to begin in the next life to become more like God. We are not simply waiting to get started with the process.

66

We are in it here and now. The implications of this are many, and there is time here to suggest only a few relevant to suffering.

If we are to become more like God, we must experience and understand the reality of physical law. Nobody in our world or in God's universe is manipulating mass, energy, motion, gravity, or quantum leaps so that they have no more reality than a TV movie or some imaginary adventure. For God, these matters of quantum leaps and mass and motion are real, and for us they are real. God functions according to laws that we are experiencing and trying to learn here. We have many scriptures indicating that our God is a God of law, and we are coming in contact with the same kind of laws He understands. Laws are real for Him, and the same laws are real for us. If they were not, we would have either incomprehensible chaos or the kind of existence which Lucifer offered.

Important to our experience is the reality of operations we can learn to depend upon and predict. Where would we be if gravity were inconsistent and we tried to sit down? Where would we be if gravity were working for some of us and not for others? Yet, when a child falls out of a high window, some wish gravity were not in effect at the moment, or suppose that God is using it to cause suffering, or look to Him to stop it. The same thing occurs with other laws of mass and motion. We want to drive to the grocery store or across the country, but the same laws of motion and mass that take us on these trips can result in accidents that disfigure people for life or leave them helpless in bed for thirteen years unable to move. We live with natural law.

Nobody is manipulating every human decision that would affect every human experience. If God did, we would have the kind of existence now that Lucifer offered permanently. For God, the agency and real existence of other souls is of prime value, value that exceeds any reason for His arbitrarily controlling all they experience and become. God does not make Himself the only reality, or the only source of reality.

"All truth is independent in that sphere in which God has placed it, to act for itself, as all intelligence also; otherwise there is no existence." (D&C 93:30.) We cannot exist without agency and its results. Neither can we become like God if we think others must be deprived of their agency so that we can be ourselves. We are not coddled toddlers in playschool or Disneyland; we are not preparing to meet reality some day. We are in it here and now.

Soon after I learned to read, I discovered folk tales and myths on a bottom shelf in the public library and devoured all that were there. Heroes and heroines were kind and brave, sharing bread with persons much uglier and very different from themselves; they were able to ride the wind east of the sun and west of the moon, and they met mountains and forests and giants and persons who could turn them to stone, and they would emerge always triumphant and happy. I was one of them and walked to school disguised as an ordinary Canadian girl in the early 1940s and thought myself kind and brave. I could meet those things and would, as the people in the stories did. I didn't know then what it was really like to be turning into stone, so to speak, or what it was like trying to swim beyond my strength, but I know now. Though I would certainly share my bread with ugly old hags or anyone else who was starving, I didn't understand compassion for someone hurting me in their own ignorance. I thought only evil persons could hurt me. The folktales were imaginary; life is real.

There is a fragment of Isaiah which illuminates the matter for me. It is better in context with surrounding chapters and best in context with all scripture but is useful even alone:

"Whom shall he teach knowledge? and whom shall he make to understand doctrine? them that are weaned from the milk, and drawn from the breasts.

"For precept must be upon precept, precept upon precept; line upon line, line upon line; here a little, and there a little:

"For with stammering lips and another tongue will he speak to this people.

"To whom he said, This is the rest wherewith ye may cause the weary to rest; and this is the refreshing: yet they would not hear.

"But the word of the Lord was unto them precept upon precept, precept upon precept; line upon line, line upon line;

here a little, and there a little; that they might go, and fall backward, and be broken, and snared, and taken." (Isaiah 28:9–13.) Why would He speak to us in a way that would let us "fall backward, and be broken, and snared, and taken"? For many years the passage puzzled me. I couldn't understand it. And yet, I think, if we are to understand God we must understand that passage.

I learned much about it one day in sacrament meeting, not from anything I heard but from watching a little boy playing in the row ahead of me. He had a quiet book open to a page with colored shapes—a purple square, an orange circle, red rectangle, green triangle, and on top of these, attached with Velcro, matching shapes and colors. The boy was clearly inexperienced. He pulled off all the shapes, then stuck a purple square on a green triangle, pulled his father's knee, and beamed up at him in utter delight because he had put a purple square on a green triangle and it stayed there. The father looked down, saw the mistake, shook his head, and turned his attention back to the speaker. The boy pulled the purple square off the green triangle, stuck it on an orange circle, pulled his father's knee, and beamed up at him with utter joy and delight. The father looked down, saw the mistake, shook his head, and turned back to the speaker. The boy pulled off the purple square and put it on a purple square, *discovered* the match, pulled his father's knee, and beamed up at him in utter delight. The father nodded and turned back to the speaker, and the boy began to experiment with the removable green triangle.

Of course, this is not a perfect metaphor for our experience with suffering or with God, but it suggests much to me in conjunction with the Isaiah passage. The boy was learning about shapes and colors, not just about being a good boy and pleasing his father by matching the right shapes and colors. Shapes and colors, useful though they be, were part of more comprehensive matters he was learning: he *can* learn, ignorance or mistakes need not be indelible, he is becoming himself, he is not the circumference of everyone else's universe, there is delight in discovery and invention, some "utter" joys are better than others, and so forth. The learning was his own, and he was taking part in creating as well as discovering that which he learned.[11]

Beyond the specifics of suffering, we too are being "weaned from the milk and drawn from the breasts" and are agents learning comprehensive matters, however brief, painful, or severely restricted earth experience might be. Even an infant born yesterday and dead of starvation or abuse within a week will experience physical reality, the quantum leaps, elements, motions, or processes which constitute physical existence. Even such an infant experiences something of how agents can affect each other and be affected by each other. Even such an ignorant child discovers that with God's help one can survive pain, imbecility, anguish, or death, and transcend them. What we meet in the way of suffering is far more important than purple squares, but we too are discovering that we can learn, and that we can take help from our Father in order that we might survive.

The history of the earth, the history of religion, is the history of human problems with understanding our Father in Heaven. We have the verse from Deuteronomy which says that if we seek the Lord with all our hearts, He will not forsake us. We have also, in the Twenty-second Psalm and in the words of Christ on the cross, "Why hast thou forsaken me?" Can we trust God? Is He a reliable help in times of trouble?

In response to such questions, some vigorously nod their heads, some look doubtful, some vigorously shake their heads, and some go to sleep. Our perceptions are not identical. God is not making them identical. He is not the only source of our understanding of Him or our relationship with Him. We take part in creating the understanding and the relationship. He invites us to come to *know* Him, not just to know about Him. The way to know Him better is to become more like Him.

If we are to find help from scriptures in this process, we must read them all in context with the writers' own language and understanding, and choose what is most important and most meaningful.[12] If we take some writings, we may look to God only for vengeance, fury, and infliction of suffering when we make any mistake or are in need of help. But I believe other writings are more expressive of LDS belief in the love of Elohim and Jehovah, Their love, Their relationship with us, and Their preservation and enhancement of our agency. For example:

"For I am persuaded, that neither death, nor life, nor angels, nor principalities, nor powers, nor things present, nor things to come,

"Nor height, nor depth, nor any other creature, shall be able to separate us from the love of God, which is in Christ Jesus our Lord." (Romans 8:38–39.)

"For we have not an high priest which cannot be touched with the feeling of our infirmities; but was in all points tempted like as we are, yet without sin.

"Let us therefore come boldly unto the throne of grace, that we may obtain mercy, and find grace to help in time of need." (Hebrews 4:15–16.)

"Ye were also in the beginning with the Father; that which is Spirit, even the Spirit of truth;

"And truth is knowledge of things as they are, and as they were, and as they are to come;

"And whatsoever is more *or less* than this is the spirit of that wicked one who was a liar from the beginning." (D&C 93:23–24; italics added.)

"He doeth not anything save it be for the benefit of the world; for he loveth the world.

" . . . he inviteth them all to come unto him and partake of his goodness; and he denieth none that come unto him, black and white, bond and free, male and female; and he remembereth the heathen; and all are alike unto God, both Jew and Gentile." (2 Nephi 26:24, 33.)

I know the love of God. It is one of the very few things I do know with absolute certainty. I think suffering on this earth is an indication of God's trust, God's love. I think it is an indication that God does not want us to be simply obedient children playing forever under His hand, but wants us able to become more like Himself. In order to do that we have to know reality. We have to be real ourselves and not dependent on externals. If we are to be like God, we cannot live forever in fear that we may meet something that will scare us or that will hurt us. We have to be able, as He is able, to meet what comes of others' agency, and of living in a lawful universe that allows creation of a habitable planet only when it allows also the difficulties that come in natural operations of such a planet.

We exist now as adolescents between ignorance and full truth, with real interactions among ourselves and the universe more numerous and complex than we yet observe or comprehend. It is within this context that I trust God and His commandments. I do not believe I could do it within the traditional framework where His love and power are supposed to keep us from pain or struggle if we are good. Neither could I find it easy to trust Him if I believed Him to make a habit of manipulating natural law and other persons to give me just what I need to test or teach me—in other words, to make me the center of the world without regard to other persons' agency or experience, and without regard to consistent, knowable law. In LDS theology, I believe, it is the *large* context for *all* humans that gives meaning to suffering. Within the context of LDS theology, I find hope for understanding and changing what I can, but also hope for transcending what I cannot: "Here is my dragon now, here is my magician who might turn me to stone, but I am able with God's help to be myself. I'm able to hurt and survive."

Some of the most difficult questions about suffering are why does God seem to intervene at some times but not others, and why should we pray for His protection. There are times we just have to say, "I don't know," and then trust God. I find this more satisfying within the context I've suggested than within traditional theologies; however, it is within the *traditional* framework that many LDS persons ask questions about suffering and God's part in it. Whatever they may say they believe about law or human agency, when the anguish comes, many LDS believers look to Jepthah's version of God and His power. In LDS theology, the power, goodness, and love of God as defined in traditional theologies are not the issues at question. Our being alive and meeting the suffering are evidence of His power, goodness, and love.

The real question is what is God's present relationship with us? I believe He loves us for ourselves, not only for Himself. I believe He is our help, our guide, the means of our present existence, our comforter, but I believe these things must be understood in a larger context than may be immediately apparent. When Elijah calls for rain to end local drought, the writer of his story does not discuss relevant necessary changes in large weather systems circling the earth, or the results of them for India or Japan. (See 1 Kings 18.)

God's power is real. The power of faith is real—it is not that God arbitrarily awards help to a person good enough to have sufficient faith, but that the faith itself is power.[13] Physical laws inherent in the universe are also real. God has repeatedly urged that we ask His help, with faith that He will do what is good. In every case, His definition of what is good is a matter of truth, and law, not arbitrary whim. We may not comprehend all the specifics, or all the interactions involved, but we can understand the theological context within which the fragments occur.

Knowing that we can stumble or fall, knowing that some do not have the gospel, or lack freedom or capacities—in other words, knowing our various limitations here—I find sense in LDS doctrine that our learning goes on after this life, and that when we fall, it need not be permanent. Many causes and effects of suffering are evident in our sense of who we are and what we can do about it. Because of our ignorance and inexperience, we are hampered by things we don't understand and also by things we assume we do understand. What other persons have taught us, whatever their intentions, may hamper as much as help us. One of my prayers to my Father is that my children will be healed of my ignorance and will not bear forever the difficulties caused by things I have mistakenly done or not done as a parent. As I think of the atonement of Christ, it seems to me that if our sins are to be forgiven, the results of them must be erased. If my mistakes are to be forgiven, other persons must be healed from any effects of them. In the same way, if other persons are to be released by the atonement, then we must be healed from their mistakes. I think that is an essential part of understanding God's gift: He did not make a plan whereby we simply prove ourselves already right or wrong. Rather, we must make sense of the fact that who we are and who we become is not wholly dependent on where we are now, and on never having made a mistake. Christ's atonement makes it possible for us to go through the meeting of reality, the falling, the hungering, the screaming, the crawling on the floor, the being disfigured and scarred for life psychologically or physically, and still survive and transcend it. If that were not true, then our whole universe would have no meaning, and we had just as well be what Lucifer suggested, simply obedient robots.

I know the goodness of God, and I also know the hurts of this life. Of the very few things I truly know, the most certain, drawn from the most vivid and inexpressible experience of my life, is this: God is love, and our becoming so is what matters. I pray we may gain courage and faith to affirm the choice we made, to remember that we are active and alive and meeting suffering here because God knew we could and because we believed we could.

Let us choose well the theology with which we frame our experience. Let us trust ourselves and God, asking continually for the help which is good. Let us love each other, mourn with each other, and sacrifice fear for courage. Let us seek reality and truth, forgiving ourselves and each other, learning to help ourselves and each other as we can. Let us become more like our God, who is good.

Notes

1. From a personal letter to the author.
2. Individual interpretation and breadth of context affect the model to be drawn from any specific verse of scripture.
3. Compare the story of Jephthah with Greek accounts of Iphigenia and King Midas. Though plots in the stories are similar, the tellers' contexts, focuses, and theologies differ, as will those of their readers.
4. Giordano Bruno, *The Heroic Frenzies,* trans. and ed. Paul Eugene Memmo, Jr. (Chapel Hill: University of North Carolina Press, 1965), p. 122.

5. One of many reasons for this is that humans have traditionally been considered to have no existence except that given them here by God—i.e., they are new creatures with no prior existence, created by God from nothing, and different from Him *in kind*. It would therefore be unthinkable that a human might become as He is, might make a leap from one species of creature to another, so to speak. It would be pretentious and prideful for the created to claim true kinship with the Creator. Compare John 5:18.

6. Such an exercise must of necessity be limited in scope. In "Science and the Citizen," *Scientific American*, August 1986, page 62, a discussion of events preceding the *Challenger* explosion begins with this paragraph:

   "In its final report the presidential commission charged with examining the explosion of the space shuttle *Challenger* identifies the design flaw that caused the accident and describes in detail the events leading up to the tragedy. It does not describe the underlying causes, within the organization of the National Aeronautics and Space Administration, that made it possible for serious dangers to be ignored."

   Nor does the report describe underlying causes of the particular organization and decision-making processes at NASA.

   If one takes a linear view of "causes" and "effects," one must go far beyond recorded history to discover all steps which have affected any subsequent event in any way. One must examine a more complex array of interactions than any human can catalogue. Consider, for example, the difficulty of tracing a traffic accident back to the invention of the wheel and then trying to figure out all that helped get the wheel invented. Then consider all interactions with other factors—for example, the morning toothbrushing that affected the time, to the second, that one of the affected persons reached the intersection at which the accident occurred.

7. See 1 Corinthians 13:9–12 in context.

8. See, for example, Doctrine and Covenants 93:29–30; Abraham 3:18, 26–28; Moses 4:1–4; Revelation 12:7–9; Doctrine and Covenants 29:36; and Wilford Woodruff's record of Joseph Smith's King Follett Discourse, available in *The Words of Joseph Smith*, comp. and ed. Andrew F. Ehat and Lyndon W. Cook (Salt Lake City, Utah: Bookcraft, 1981), pp. 343-48.

   If it were God who originally created our personal capabilities and quiddities, or if they originally came about by any kind of "chance," then any differences among us, and results of them, must ultimately be attributed to God or to chance. We could not be responsible for what we are or what we do. If we are choosers now, we must always have been choosers, within the constraints that current knowledge, understanding, or abilities would allow.

9. "What kind of weapons did they use in the war in heaven?" a nine-year-old girl once asked in a Sunday School class I was teaching.

10. Consider the model for Judgment Day suggested by such verses as Alma 29:4–5. If we are to be capable of choosing to become more like God, then we must also know enough to reject it if we do not want what godhood actually is.

11. Compare this concluding paragraph from the unsigned introductory note in *Japanese Haiku* (Mount Vernon, New York: Peter Pauper Press, 1955):

    "One final word: The *haiku* is not expected to be always a complete or even a clear statement. The reader is supposed to add to the words his own associations and imagery, and thus to become a co-creator of his own pleasure in the poem. The publishers hope their readers may here co-create such pleasure for themselves!"

12. This is suggested by such verses as: 2 Nephi 31:3; Isaiah 55:8–9; Doctrine and Covenants 29:31–34; Doctrine and Covenants 130:16–17.

13. See, for example, Jacob 4:6; Enos 8; 3 Nephi 17:8; Ether 3, 12:12–21; Moroni 7:37; 10:7.

The Many Facets of Grief

DEANNE FRANCIS

I heard a weak cry as the doctor quickly clamped the cord and placed the tiny, unfinished baby into the open isolette. The respiratory therapist and I dried and stimulated the baby girl, gave her oxygen, and watched as she struggled to breathe. Her chest caved in nearly to her backbone with each inhalation, and a pushing groan accompanied each exhalation. She lay limp and slightly blue as we tried to help her breathe with a bag and mask, finally resorting to placing a tube in her trachea.

At the door of the delivery room, an anxious father paled as he watched the things we were doing to his daughter. This was not what he had in mind when he had contemplated his impending fatherhood. From the delivery room, I heard the mother cry in anguish, "Is she all right; is she going to live?" I looked down at the baby and wished I could offer the mother more hope. This baby, only slightly bigger than a pound of butter, was born over three months too soon. While we had saved other babies that small, the odds were against her.

When the neonatologist arrived, I went to talk to the parents, whose names were Dave and Sue. Explaining the situation briefly, I invited them both to come down to the intensive care nursery to visit their daughter as soon as possible. We pushed the isolette close to the delivery table on our way to the nursery so that Sue could reach in and gently stroke the baby's hand, no bigger than her own thumbnail.

Deanne Francis, a registered nurse with a B.S. degree in nursing, works with the newborn intensive care unit at Utah Valley Regional Medical Center. She has served on the medical advisory board of the March of Dimes for ten years and has taught prenatal classes for more than two decades. A frequent speaker for university and civic groups, Sister Francis has been a Relief Society president and has worked in many callings in Primary and Young Women. She is the mother of six children.

They named their baby Ashley. We taped her name over the front of the isolette and hung up the pink booties they bought. Over the next few days we watched Dave and Sue undergo the emotional roller coaster parents ride with a sick newborn. One day the news was encouraging; the next, we had a crisis. We listened as Dave and Sue searched to find answers for the premature birth, became angry that this had happened to them, bargained with God for Ashley's life, and became impatient with the staff over insignificant things.

Twelve days after the baby's birth, I knelt on the floor in front of Sue with a box of Kleenex between us as she held her tiny daughter for what would be the first and last time. This would not be one of our success stories. Ashley was dying, and there was nothing we could do but allow this family some time together.

Many people have asked me how nurses handle situations like this. I don't know about anyone else, but after twenty-four years, I still cry—every time.

Birth and Death

Nurses are very frequently present at both birth and death, and they spend a good deal of time endeavoring to instill dignity and comfort into both of these events. Birth is usually a joyous occasion and obviously is much more easily handled than death. But when these two events happen in close proximity, the grief is particularly acute since the death of a baby seems so incomprehensible. It is the difficult job of those of us who work with sick newborns in an intensive care nursery to manage birth, anticipatory grief, and sometimes death, within hours or days of each other.

In fact, nurses probably witness death more often than any other group of people except soldiers in wartime. It is necessary to accept death and particularly the grief process which affects both the dying and those who will be left behind.

Death, like birth, is a fact of life. For some it is sudden, for some a lengthy and painful process. For some it comes almost before life has begun, for others in the bloom of adulthood, and for others in the infirmity of old age. But it comes. Some fight it and struggle against it to the last moment. Some pray for death as a release. All of us are, in fact, dying. It's just that some are dying faster than others. Fortunately, we do not choose the timing and circumstances of our own or a loved one's death. For what would we choose? When would be a good time? Gratefully, that is the Lord's prerogative.

The Universal Nature of Grief

I suppose that anyone asked to discuss the process of grief wonders what qualifications one must have to speak on that particular subject. In contemplating this, I concluded that anyone who has lived long enough is qualified to discuss death with some feeling and insight, since we all experience a loss of some type sooner or later.

My own experience with grief is not unique. My husband and I have had to cope with the loss of all four of our parents. My father had to return home from serving as a mission president with a very severe brain disease that accounted for his suicide a year later at age fifty. My mother, at age sixty-two, developed a similar but unrelated brain disease that claimed her in just twelve weeks. I have had five miscarriages and one child born with a serious birth defect. These are not unusual experiences, and I relate them briefly to point out the universality of sad experiences. They are all part of mortality, and everyone can relate similar experiences that elicited a grief response. We each deal with these difficult aspects of mortality in individual and unique ways which involve choice and accountability.

All of us agreed to come here and to accept our earthly life with all its joys, happiness, and peace, as well as its grief, illness, loss, and death. But when actually faced with the loss of a loved one, with loss of a body part or function, or with divorce or separation, some of us respond by losing faith, placing bitter blame, or sinking into paralyzing depression. In doing so, we discover that we may have been giving only lip service to accepting the conditions of mortality.

What Shall I Say?

It is so hard to know what to say or how to help a person

immersed in grief. Last year, my husband and I took our daughter with us to the viewing of one of her friends who had been killed in a car accident along with both his parents and one brother. "I want to go because I feel so bad," she said, "but what shall I say to his sisters?" I could only advise her that caring enough to go and saying anything she felt in her heart was better than staying away and saying nothing.

What is the best help to offer a bereaved and grieving friend? What can be said to parents who have just had a baby born with a birth defect? All their plans and hopes and dreams for that child must be revised. What support can be given when a child is going to live with a severe defect that will be more difficult than death? What can a husband do to help a beloved wife who is dying? How will an athlete deal with the loss of a leg? Each of these people will go through a grief process that can be modified and resolved more completely with adequate support. The ways in which human beings deal with impending death depends upon sex, age, wisdom, circumstances, culture, personality, and faith. Those left behind also respond in different ways. There is choice involved in our reaction to death and to dying — the same as in all other areas of life. In choosing how we will deal with bereavement, though, we need to understand the elements common to those who pass through it.

Elements of Grief

Although grief involves phases, there is no "correct" order or time span for each of them. Grief is very personal and individual. It helps, however, to know these phases and to recognize them in ourselves and others as we face a loss of some kind or as we try to help someone else face a loss. We also need to recognize that the feelings and suffering involved in each of these phases need not be permanent and that they can be modified in a positive manner in many ways.

Shock and denial. Inasmuch as grief is personal, let us imagine that you have just lost the person closest to you or have just been told you have terminal cancer. After the initial waves of shock and numbness have passed, you will then hear yourself say, "Oh no, this can't be happening to me," or, "There must be a mistake. It can't be true."

It is difficult to comprehend the enormity of what has happened. Friends and neighbors rally around, and visitors are many. Condolence calls are difficult for both parties, but they are made out of love and concern. You must be able to allow other people to help. They will offer, and it will help if you make suggestions about what things could be done.

Accepting assistance from understanding professionals can often be of great benefit at this point. Doctors, nurses, bishops, funeral directors, members of Hospice, or medical social workers are usually good counselors, having encountered this aspect of grief so many times. The support available through self-help groups is typically underestimated and ignored. If you can find someone who has been through your particular experience and has become a stronger person as a result, talking with that person will give you great insight.

It is during this stage that preparations for burial must be made. Planning a viewing, writing an obituary, and asking people to participate in a funeral are difficult, but all these things have great therapeutic value. It is the beginning of being able to say goodbye. It brings the support of friends and provides a goal or objective to work toward. It also provides for a last, loving tribute and declaration of love.

Following all these customary procedures, the thing that usually happens is the support group leaves. The Relief Society sisters, the family, and your friends all go back home and leave you with your grief and your loneliness, except in rare instances. There are a few remarkable people who know when they are needed most. I will be forever grateful to Bill and Lou Homer, who did not go home and forget. For thirteen years after my father died, they called my mother almost every Friday and took her somewhere with them. This practice probably would have continued for many more years if my mother had not died.

Anger. After the "not me" stage has passed, your next thought may be, "Why me?" "What have I done wrong to deserve this?" You may begin to search for a place to lay the blame, and you will be angry. You may be angry at the need for nurses and doctors to care for your baby. You may be angry at doctors and nurses who couldn't save your loved one. Perhaps your anger will be directed at the one who caused the accident or toward the God who "allowed it to happen." You may even be angry at the one who has died for "deserting" you.

If you direct this anger at your mate, it can cause tremendous marital strife. "If only you hadn't gone jogging yesterday, this baby would not have been born prematurely." "You should never have let her drive the car out on the freeway." If you can talk about your grief, share your feelings, and understand each other's deep mourning, you will come through the process with a stronger marriage and a deeper love. Even if there is real fault, enlarging your mate's guilt will not improve the situation. It is no wonder that the divorce rate is high among couples who have had a baby in intensive care. The stress is incredible.

Guilt. Few survivors of tragedies escape without some feelings of guilt, some real and some imagined, so don't be surprised if you begin laying some blame at your own feet. "If only I had taken him to the doctor sooner...." "I shouldn't have put him in a nursing home." "I should have said, 'I love you.' "

You will find that like everyone else, you have 20/20 hindsight. Unfortunately, your foresight is not nearly so good. When guilt begins to gnaw and twist your soul, ask yourself this question: "If I had this person back, could I be sure I'd never make another mistake?" If you are the one dying, ask yourself, "If I could live a little longer, could I guarantee I'd live perfectly?" Most of us cannot be sure that we would behave any better or be any more considerate or loving if given another chance.

I can tell you from experience that there is a tremendous amount of guilt connected with suicide. If you are the one left behind, you will ask yourself, as I did, "What did we do to make him want to take his own life?" I learned that no one can control the behavior of another person. I also learned through watching my father's brain disease progress that he was unable to control his own behavior. How grateful I am that a wiser One than I will be the judge of these things.

Depression. When the numbness and shock wear off, when the rage has exhausted itself and the questions still are unanswered, despair tends to take over. If you are the one dying, you may begin to bargain, usually with God. "Heavenly Father, if I can only be spared, I will pay a full tithing and live a perfect life." In the case where someone you love has died, you may finally be able to say, "This dreadful thing has really happened to me. What do I do now?"

This is the time when you will need support the most. It will help to talk and to stay active. Your discussions may be rambling and repetitive, so you will need a very caring friend who knows how to listen in a nonjudgmental way without offering platitudes or too much good advice, no matter how well-meaning. You will also need someone who will not allow you to become so steeped in your own misery that you do nothing but vegetate and dwell on your loss. You may resent this person's trying to keep you involved in the things you have always loved, but if you can rouse yourself to participate in life's activities one day at a time, you will find that it will get easier and more enjoyable. You may also find that you have gone backwards into one of the previous stages and must repeat the process of progression. Just when you thought you had conquered your anger, for example, you will wake one morning to find yourself filled with resentment all over again. Simply recognizing that regression is not unusual may make it easier to bear.

Acceptance. When you have reached this stage, you will have come to terms with your grief and your loss and will have achieved some measure of peace. You will be able to face the issue squarely and say, "I'm ready to go," or "I'm ready to accept this loss, as hard as it is, and go on with my life." Unfortunately, some never reach this stage but become arrested in one of the other stages where bitterness, anger, and depression can go on for a lifetime.

In my opinion, and in the opinion of many researchers, it is faith that is the most powerful tool in helping a person reach a calm acceptance of death and dying. Faith gives strength from a higher power than we mere mortals can provide. Prayer and the scriptures do provide answers. They provide comfort and solace. Faith in God and the plan of salvation provides hope and assurance that death is also a beginning, a birth, rather than the end.

Taking Advice from Those Who Have Been There

With permission, I use the suggestions and comments that were given to me by five remarkable people who have had to face overwhelming bereavement, death, and pain. The things that happened to these people are not unique; they are things that could happen to any or all of us. The uniqueness is the courageous and positive manner in which these individuals met their test. That's what mortality is, after all—a test. The kind of tests we face here are not important. The way in which we choose to face them and what we become because of them are important eternally.

Janna. A nurse friend of mine went to check on her baby and discovered that he was dead—a victim of crib death. Several months later, looking back, she commented that husbands and wives tend to grieve differently. "Men," she said, "may need to cry but find it difficult." She also noted that among those who suffer loss there is a tendency to try to meet society's expectations of how we are supposed to act. Always we hear the admonitions, "Be brave" or "Don't cry." Crying is healing in process. It's like cleansing a wound so it will heal. "Crying helps get the sad and the mad out of you. Crying is like gentle melting."[1]

The nicest thing we may be able to do for a grieving friend is to allow tears. My friend also suggested that in expressing sorrow over the loss of a child, it is better not to make the comment, "It is good that you have other children" or "Well, you will always be able to have other children." That child was an individual, loved for his own particular personality and qualities, and no other child can compensate for the loss of that individual.

Kay. Another friend of mine was left a widow with six small children. Her loss and sadness were immense, but she gathered her children around her and said, "We are not going to fall apart. We will carry on the same as if Dad were here. We will be a family."

She spoke with each child individually and listened to each one's feelings about the loss of their father. She was able to put aside her own grief long enough to help each of her children face the issue squarely. In doing so, it meant she had to face the issue also, and that included going back to work as an attorney to support her family. She has done this with vigor and humor, and I salute her. She realized that children, too, go through the grief process and have needs in their sorrow that should not be overlooked. Helping children with grief is not easy. "The best care we can give you is not to protect you from pain but to support you through it."[2]

Katy. While serving as a Relief Society president, I had the privilege of helping to care for a young wife and mother as she slowly wasted away with cancer. She had chosen to stay home rather than be hospitalized, and more than anything she wanted to die with dignity. We talked of many things in the hours I was with her, and those hours will always be precious to me. I well remember many of her comments. "Take the time to do the things that are important," she said. When I asked her what she considered important, she said, "I would like to look at one more oak tree, and go out with a friend for a milkshake." We arranged for her to do these things.

She commented that euphemisms do not help. "Everything will be all right" is meaningless to a person who knows she is dying. Everything is not all right. One day she listened patiently when a visitor spent a great deal of time saying, in effect, "You've got it bad, but so-and-so has got it worse." Then followed a long discussion of someone else's illness. When the visitor left, Katy said, "Do you think I should feel compensated because other people have had worse experiences?" Probably such comments are not helpful.

Gayle and Brent. My closest friend lost her mother during heart surgery. Both she and her husband commented that they appreciated anyone and everyone who called or came by and offered well-meaning words. They agreed that saying nothing about the person who has died is worse than putting your foot in your mouth and that visitors who avoided the subject of their beloved mother caused more pain than anything that might have been said.

My friend said that she could think of little else at the time, and she most appreciated those who shared memories with her about her mother and her life. Those shared memories become treasures to remember. Dietrich Bonhoeffer said, "We must not wallow in our memories or surrender to them, just as we don't gaze all the time at a valuable present. But get it out from time to time, and for the rest hide it away as a treasure we know is there all the time. Treated this way, the past can give us lasting joy and inspiration."[3]

Michelle. Finally, I offer the insight of the young woman whose parents and two brothers were killed in a car accident. She and her two sisters were the only ones who remained in her immediate family. "I am sure," she said, "that there is an explanation and a reason for this." That says a great deal. We, with our limited knowledge, may not understand the reasons for things happening the way they do or at the time they do. With our finite understanding of time, it is difficult for us to truly judge when a person's time here on earth is finished. I think Michelle understood that we must find purpose and acceptance in the difficult trials of life and realize that the great eternal plan has beauty we cannot see now.

Enduring in Faith

Mary V. Hill, in concluding her book *Angel Children: Those Who Die Before Accountability*, observed that after the death of her son, she became a different person:

"I believe that I have deeper faith in and love for our Father in Heaven and His Son Jesus Christ than ever before. I feel that my soul has been tried in the refiner's fire and has emerged more purified. I know now that my faith is built upon rock, because it did not crash around me in the strength of the storm as it would have done had it been built upon sand. I have watched my husband, my children, my parents, my brothers and sisters, and my friends all grow in their understanding of the gospel and the meaning of life and death on this earth since little Stephen was born. Who then can say that little Stephen's illness, his brief life of three and a half months, and his death were useless, meaningless tragedies? I believe with all my heart that his life here was a mission to teach us great truths, a sacred trust for us to cherish and share with others."[4]

Dave and Sue had a great advantage over some of the other anguished parents I have watched in our intensive care nursery. They understood and truly lived the gospel. In all their activities, they had relied on the Lord for guidance and help, and He had not deserted them, nor did He as their baby died. They cried and dressed her in a pink doll's dress, took a picture to remember, and invited grandparents and other relatives to join them for a special family night. They prayed for Ashley and for the strength to endure a parting. Underlying their grief was the tremendous faith that they would see and hold their daughter again. This family went through all the stages and facets of grief, but they emerged from the process as stronger, wiser, and more resilient people. To be determined to do this constitutes faithful endurance.

There is spiritual and practical help for those who face death, divorce, amputation, or the loss of a loved one. Love, assurance, and acceptance are God's gift to all who earnestly seek Him after the anguish has passed. We are expected to endure to the end, whenever that is. "We hope all things, we have endured many things, and hope to be able to endure all things"—but not without help, comfort, and guidance. (Articles of Faith 1:13.) By sharing these things and experiencing these things we gain wisdom and peace.

In the Gospel of John, there is great solace and comfort:

"Peace I leave with you, my peace I give unto you: not as the world giveth, give I unto you. Let not your heart be troubled, neither let it be afraid." (John 14:27.)

"In my Father's house are many mansions: if it were not so, I would have told you. I go to prepare a place for you." (John 14:2.)

Notes

1. Pat Schwiebert and Paul Kirk, *When Hello Means Goodbye: A Guide for Parents Whose Child Dies Before Birth, at Birth, or Shortly after Birth,* ed. Perinatal Loss Project, rev. 2d ed. (Portland, Oreg.: Perinatal Loss Project, 1985), p. 15.
2. Schwiebert and Kirk, *When Hello Means Goodbye,* p. 24.
3. Schwiebert and Kirk, *When Hello Means Goodbye,* p. 24.
4. Bountiful, Utah: Horizon Publishers, 1973, pp. 58-59.

Other References

Buntin, Kathleen Rawlings. *The Living Half.* Salt Lake City: Deseret Book, 1984.

Dunn, Paul H., and Richard M. Eyre. *The Birth That We Call Death.* Salt Lake City: Bookcraft, 1976.

Hill, Norman C. *When the Road Gets Rough.* Salt Lake City: Bookcraft, 1986.

Jensen, Amy Hillyard. *Healing Grief.* Evanston, Ill.: Medic Publishing Co., 1980.

The Effects on Women of
Recent Changes in Divorce Laws

STEPHEN J. BAHR

*D*uring the past twenty-five years, family life in the
United States has changed dramatically. The rate of
childbearing has decreased, female employment has increased,
and divorce and remarriage have become much more common. As a result, today's families are much smaller than in the
past, and we have more dual-earner families, single-parent
families, and remarried families.

These social changes have been accompanied by significant
changes in the laws that regulate marriage, contraception, abortion, and divorce. The changes in divorce laws have had considerable consequences for women.

When one talks of changes in the law, most people think
of changes in legislation. Legislation, however, is only one
important way laws are made. Another equally important type
of law is case law made by courts. Statutes are often broad,
and courts make law when they interpret the law by applying
it to specific situations. Court rulings on abortion illustrate well
how courts make law. Before 1973 it was a criminal offense
for a woman to obtain an abortion, except when her life was
in danger. The United States Supreme Court radically changed
abortion law in 1973 when it ruled that the fetus is not a person
and that states cannot prohibit abortions during the first trimes-
ter of pregnancy. (Roe v. Wade 410 U.S. 113, 1973.)

*Stephen J. Bahr, the director of the Family and Demographic
Research Institute and a professor of sociology at Brigham Young
University, earned his Ph.D. from Washington State University. He
has served as president of the Utah Council on Family Relations and
as associate editor of the* Journal of Marriage and the Family *and the*
Journal of Family Issues. *His Church callings have included stake
high councilor, Scoutmaster, Sunday School teacher, and stake physical activities specialist.*

An important characteristic of divorce law is that it is state law. According to the Tenth Amendment of the United States Constitution, any power not specifically given to the federal government rests in the states. Consequently, the federal government cannot legislate marriage and divorce laws, and divorce cases are handled in state courts. Only when cases are appealed to the United States Supreme Court is the federal government involved directly in divorce law.

Two major changes have occurred in marital dissolution laws during the past two decades. First, no-fault divorce laws have been passed in most states. Second, the laws have become gender neutral in response to the equal rights movement. These two changes need to be carefully assessed as to their consequences for women.

No-Fault Divorce

Trends. In early America divorce was granted because of some serious marital misconduct such as adultery, desertion, or extreme physical cruelty. The innocent party (plaintiff) obtained a divorce from the wrongdoer (defendant) as compensation. Divorce was denied unless there was marital misconduct, and it was illegal for a husband and a wife to mutually agree to a divorce.

Gradually the grounds for divorce were expanded, with "mental cruelty" included as a ground for divorce. The demand for divorce gradually increased, and the meaning of "mental cruelty" was broadened to include a variety of negative behaviors.

As divorce became more common, fault laws came under increasing criticism for two major reasons. First, fault laws required one spouse to charge the other with misconduct. The natural response is to make a counter charge, which invokes additional charges and responses. The result is the escalation of conflict, and a stressful situation is made worse. (Clark, 1976.) Second, it is usually unrealistic to label only one spouse as the guilty party, since rarely is one spouse solely responsible for the marital problems. Even if one spouse is primarily at fault,

90

usually it does not help the situation to focus only on that misconduct.

The dissatisfaction with fault laws resulted in the passage of "no-fault" divorce legislation in most states. In 1967 New York became the first state to enact no-fault legislation by adding "living separate and apart" as a ground for divorce. A New York couple may now obtain a divorce if they have lived apart for a year, without stating that either is at fault. California added to its grounds for divorce "irreconcilable differences" in 1970, and Utah did so in 1987. To divorce, a couple under this law need only stipulate that they have "irreconcilable differences," without laying blame on anyone.

Today fifty states have passed some type of no-fault divorce statute. (Freed and Walker, 1986.) In fourteen states "irreconcilable differences" or "irretrievable breakdown" is the sole ground for divorce, and in thirty-six states individuals may choose between a fault or no-fault ground. That is, they may charge their spouse with a wrong such as adultery or cruelty, or they may assert that their marriage is irretrievably broken, without assessing fault.

Consequences. It was feared by some that no-fault laws would make divorce easier and cause an increase in divorce rates. These fears were not borne out, however. Research in a number of states has shown that divorce rates began increasing about eight years before no-fault laws were passed and that increases in divorce rates were similar for states with and without no-fault statutes. (Dixon and Weitzman, 1980; Mazur-Hart and Berman, 1977; Michael, 1978; Sell, 1979; Schoen et al., 1975; Wright and Stetson, 1978.) There is no evidence that no-fault divorce laws made divorce easier or caused an increase in the divorce rates. Divorce was easy to obtain under fault laws, such as the one in Utah where "mental cruelty" is ground for divorce. The definition of mental cruelty used by the courts is so broad that behavior exhibited in most marriages could be considered legal grounds for divorce if brought to court.

No-fault laws have reduced conflict that results in court trials. A study of divorce cases in California revealed that since the passage of no-fault laws, there has been less litigation at each stage of the legal process. (Dixon and Weitzman, 1980.) The findings suggest that removing fault has helped reduce hostility generated in the divorce process.

In summary, the change to no-fault divorce has had no effect on divorce rates but has reduced the number of divorce trials. Since trials are expensive to the parties and taxpayers, no-fault divorce appears to have saved money.

Gender Equality

Trends. The second major change in divorce laws is the movement to gender equality. At about the same time no-fault legislation was being passed, the United States Supreme Court gave a new interpretation to the Fourteenth Amendment to the Constitution. The Fourteenth Amendment was passed after the Civil War to ensure that blacks were treated equally under the law; its framers did not intend that it be applied to gender, and for over one hundred years it was not. In 1971, however, the United States Supreme Court gave it a new interpretation and said that a law that preferred males over females as executors of estates violated the equal protection clause of the Fourteenth Amendment. (Reed v. Reed, 404 U.S. 71, 1971.) A series of subsequent court cases firmly established that the Fourteenth Amendment outlaws many distinctions between males and females. (Stanley v. Illinois, 405 U.S. 645, 1972; Frantiero v. Richardson, 411 U.S. 677, 1973; Wiesenfield v. Weinburger, 420 U.S. 636, 1975; Orr v. Orr, 440 U.S. 268, 1979.) As a result of the new interpretation of the Fourteenth Amendment, many divorce laws have been changed.

One of the major changes has been in the area of child custody. Before 1971 it was assumed the mother should have custody of the children, especially if they were of "tender years." It is no longer assumed that the mother is the preferred custodian of the children. The tender years presumption has been rejected in most states, and its power has been reduced in the other states. (Freed and Foster, 1984.) More than 60 percent of the states have passed laws that equalize parental rights to child custody. At least thirty-one states have passed laws permitting custody to be shared jointly between divorcing parents. (Freed and Foster, 1984.) The law increasingly recognizes that fathers can nurture children and have the right to obtain custody.

A second major change has been to remove gender as a factor in dividing money and property. In many states laws have been passed to award alimony and support on need and ability to pay rather than on gender. In 1979 the United States Supreme Court ruled that it was unconstitutional to use gender as a criterion for alimony. (Orr v. Orr, 440 U.S. 268.) The court maintained that an Alabama law that allowed only females to receive alimony was based on outmoded sexual stereotypes and violated the equal protection clause of the Fourteenth Amendment. In California all assets acquired during the marriage must be divided equally if they are disputed.

Consequences. The changes in the laws have had little effect on child custody. As in previous years, women obtain custody of children in about nine of every ten divorce cases. There has been a slight increase in the number of husbands who receive custody and in the number of joint custody awards, although both remain relatively small in number. (Dixon and Weitzman, 1980; McGraw et al., 1982.)

The major effect of the movement toward gender equality has been to hurt women economically. Alimony and child support are being awarded less frequently, and when awarded, the amounts in real dollars are smaller than in the past. (Seal, 1979; Dixon and Weitzman, 1980; Weitzman, 1981.) The length of awards has also decreased. Rather than being viewed as a long-term entitlement for contributions to a marriage, alimony increasingly is seen as short-term compensation to help wives rehabilitate themselves economically. (Freed and Foster, 1984; Weitzman, 1981.) Today family assets are less likely to be granted exclusively to the wife than in the past. The primary asset of many marriages is the home, which in the past usually became the wife's. The new equality has changed this pattern and, in some cases, has forced the sale of the home to divide the property "equally." The net result of the movement toward gender equality has been a substantial decrease in money and property received by women who divorce. (Seal, 1979; Dixon and Weitzman, 1980; Weitzman, 1981.)

It is assumed by many that the need for alimony and support is less today than in the past because of increasing rates of employment among women. This assumption is simply incorrect. Divorced females and not divorced males are disproportionately represented among the poor, and living standards of females, but not males, decrease significantly following divorce. (Bahr, 1984; Bradbury et al., 1979; Espenshade, 1979; Weitzman, 1981.) The already precarious economic situation of divorced women has been made worse by recent changes in divorce laws.

The traditional marriage is based on a division of labor between husband and wife. The husband is the primary wage-earner and has invested in job training. The wife, rather than preparing economically, has invested herself in caring for the home and children. When such a marriage dissolves, these differences do not automatically vanish. In most cases women obtain custody of the children, and men maintain superior economic ability. Equity would require that monetary transfers be made from husband to wife; however, the recent movement toward gender equality has resulted in fewer economic transfers from husbands to wives. It is assumed that men and women are equally situated and that monetary transfers are needed only temporarily, if at all. It is also assumed that existing marital assets should be divided equally.

Since the wife usually has custody of the children, child-rearing responsibilities are not equal. Employment opportunities and wages are less for women than for men. Divorced females and males have been treated similarly economically, when in fact there are large differences between them. Real equality would demand that they be treated differently simply because they are not similarly situated.

Recent Changes

There have been several recent changes to help correct the economic inequities faced by divorced women, specifically, modifications in laws governing child support, pensions, and nonmonetary contributions.

The widespread disregard for child support is a national disgrace. Payment of child support is the exception rather than the rule, and defaults exceeded four billion in 1984. (Horowitz, 1985.) To help remedy this situation, Congress passed the Child Support Amendments of 1984 (Public Law 98-378), which require that states enact laws to do the following:

1. Establish mandatory wage withholding if support payments are a month delinquent.

2. Impose liens against real and personal property for amounts of overdue support.

3. Withhold state income tax refunds if a parent is delinquent in child support payments.

4. Make available information regarding the amount of overdue support to any consumer credit bureau.

5. Establish expedited processes within the state judicial system for obtaining and enforcing child support orders.

One of the major inequities for women has been their loss of pension at divorce. Pensions were often viewed as an individual entitlement, and the rules of many federal and private pensions precluded payment to anyone but the pension holder.

A recent California case that went to the United States Supreme Court illustrates this problem. A Mr. McCarty divorced his wife after eighteen years of marriage. According to California law, which governed their divorce, each spouse has an absolute and equal right to half interest in all community property. Community property is defined as all assets acquired during the marriage, including the pension fund. The California trial court ruled that Mr. McCarty must pay his ex-wife 45 percent of his military retirement pay, based on the eighteen years that the pension had been accruing. On appeal, the United States Supreme Court said military retirement was an individual entitlement and overturned the California court's ruling. (McCarty v. McCarty, 453 U.S. 210, 1981.) Mrs. McCarty lost all rights to her husband's retirement fund, even though she had been married to him for eighteen years.

The divorced woman whose husband had a private pension often faced a similar situation. The private pension was in her husband's name and upon divorce, no matter how long they were married, that pension was his.

Two recent laws have changed this situation. In September 1982 President Ronald Reagan signed into law the Uniformed Services Former Spouses Protection Act (Public Law 97-252). This act overturned the Supreme Court's decision in McCarty and returned to state courts the power to decide whether military retirement benefits are marital property divisible at the time of divorce. The new law recognizes the reality of the marital partnership and the contributions made by both spouses in acquiring pensions. There is no minimum duration of marriage for the parties to qualify under the act, and military personnel may designate the former spouse as beneficiary.

The situation for private pensions has been improved by the Retirement Equity Act (Public Law 98-387), which passed Congress in August 1984. Before enactment of this law, many pension plans would not pay former spouses, even if the court ordered them to. The pension was considered an individual entitlement not divisible upon divorce. The Retirement Equity Act requires that pension plans honor valid divorce court awards. Furthermore, the former spouse may collect her share as soon as her former husband reaches the pension plan's earliest retirement age, which is usually age fifty-five. It makes no difference whether he retires then or continues to work. Time and form of payments are quite flexible under the act.

One other legal trend is the recognition of nonmonetary contributions of a spouse as homemaker, parent, and contributor to the well-being of the family. These contributions do not provide income directly and are usually not given a specific monetary value. Nevertheless, they are valued services on which the family depends. It would cost a considerable amount to hire someone to provide those services, and, in that sense, they are real economic contributions. Courts are beginning to take these nonmonetary contributions into account in divorce awards. Currently thirty-three states recognize the nonmonetary contributions of a spouse to the marital assets. (Freed and

Foster, 1984.) The nonmonetary contributions of a spouse are only one factor among many used to determine awards, however, and are difficult to evaluate. Furthermore, courts change slowly and do not evaluate nonmonetary contributions realistically or consider the economic worth of lost opportunity.

The actual effects of these new laws have not yet been determined. Hopefully, the Child Support Amendments will increase the receipt of child support by custodial parents. Women should receive more equitable pension payments because of the Uniformed Services Former Spouses Protection Act and the Retirement Equity Act. The recognition of nonmonetary contributions is a promising legal trend but probably will not change divorce awards substantially in the near future.

Conclusion

In temporal terms, the family is first and foremost an economic unit. The dissolution of that unit can be difficult for women because men are usually the primary wage-earners. The economic problems of divorced women can be solved in four major ways. First, they could receive monetary payments from their former husband. Recent changes in laws regarding child support and pensions should increase payments from husbands; however, these new laws will not change the frequency with which courts award spousal support or the propensity of men to pay spousal support. Courts need to award support more frequently and in greater amounts, but courts are slow to change. Judges should be trained to assess more realistically both need and ability to pay. The economic worth of nonmonetary contributions to the marriage should be recognized by judges when they make support awards.

Second, the government could increase welfare funds to support these women. Given existing tax burdens and the size of welfare rolls, additional welfare money for divorced women is unlikely.

Third, women could receive more job training and employment opportunities. In the long run, this solution is probably the single best one for women. Even with training, however, it is difficult for women to enter the job market when they have been out of the labor force for a number of years. Training is expensive and does not guarantee a job. Furthermore, one of the major strains of divorced women is trying to earn the living and simultaneously care for the home and the children. (Bahr, 1982.)

A fourth solution for women is remarriage. The economic situation of women improves dramatically when they remarry, and about three-fourths remarry within five years of their divorce. (Bahr, 1984; Glick, 1980.)

In summary, we have seen two major changes in divorce laws during the past two decades. One has been the removal of fault as grounds for divorce. This change has had no effect on the divorce rates but has decreased the number of court trials. This trend appears beneficial for women because less litigation saves money.

The second trend has been a change to gender-neutral laws. This has had little effect on child custody. In about nine out of ten cases the woman remains the custodian of the children. Economically, these changes have been devastating for women because the frequency and amount of support awards have decreased. In the name of equality, economic inequality has resulted. Hopefully, recently passed laws regarding child support and pensions will reduce this inequality. Other ways to help solve the economic plight of divorced women are needed, particularly more realistic support awards along with job training.

References

Bahr, Stephen J. 1982. The pains and joys of divorce: a survey of Mormons. *Family Perspective* 16: 191–200.

——. 1983. Marital dissolution laws: impact of recent changes for women. *Journal of Family Issues* 4 (3): 455–66.

——. 1984. Child support: problems and prospects. *Family Perspective* 18: 85–90.

Bradbury, K., S. Danziger, E. Smolensky, and P. Smolensky. 1979. Public assistance, female headship, and economic well-being. *Journal of Marriage and the Family* 41: 519–35.

Brigner, V. M. 1982. "I put him through school . . . now he says we're finished." *Family Advocate* 4 (3): 16–19, 43–44.

Clark, M. F. 1976. Florida's no-fault divorce: is it really no-fault? *Florida State University Law Review* 4: 504–22.

Dixon, R. B., and L. J. Weitzman. 1980. Evaluating the impact of no-fault divorce in California. *Family Relations* 29: 297–307.

———. 1982. When husbands file for divorce. *Journal of Marriage and the Family* 44: 103–14.

Espenshade, T. J. 1979. The economic consequences of divorce. *Journal of Marriage and the Family* 41: 615–26.

Freed, Doris J., and Henry H. Foster. 1981. Divorce in the fifty states: an overview. *Family Law Quarterly* 14: 229–83.

———. 1984. Family law in the fifty states: an overview. *Family Law Quarterly* 17: 365–447.

Freed, Doris J., and Timothy B. Walker. 1986. Family law in the fifty states: an overview. *Family Law Quarterly* 19: 331–441.

Glick, Paul C. Remarriage: some recent changes and variations. *Journal of Family Issues* 1 (1980): 455–78.

Horowitz, Robert M. 1985. The child support amendments of 1984. *Juvenile and Family Court Journal* 36: 1–4.

McGraw, R. E., G. J. Sterin, and J. M. Davis. 1982. A case study in divorce law reform and its aftermath. *Journal of Family Law* 20: 443–87.

Michael, R. T. 1977. Why has the U.S. divorce rate doubled within the decade? Working paper N 202, Stanford, Calif.: National Bureau of Economic Research.

Mazur-Hart, S. F., and J. J. Berman. 1977. Changing from fault to no-fault divorce: an interrupted time series analysis. *Journal of Applied Social Psychology* 7: 300–312.

Schoen, R. H., N. Greenblatt, and R. B. Mielke. 1975. California's experience with nonadversary divorce. *Demography* 12: 223–43.

Seal, K. 1979. A decade of no-fault divorce: what it has meant financially for women in California. *Family Advocate* 1 (Spring) 4: 10–15.

Sell, K. D. 1979. Divorce law reform and increasing divorce rates. In *Current Issues in Marriage and the Family,* ed. J. G. Wells, pp. 290–308. New York: Macmillan.

Weitzman, L. 1981. The economics of divorce: social and economic consequences of property, alimony, and child support awards. *UCLA Law Review* 28: 1181–1268.

Wright, G. C., Jr., and D. M. Stetson. 1978. The impact of no-fault divorce law reform on divorce in American states. *Journal of Marriage and the Family* 40: 575–80.

Women of Faith in a Violent World

ANNE L. HORTON

*S*o often the view of the world of religious women is a negative one—one of reaction, victimization and mindless submission. Yet, for the Latter-day Saint woman, faith is equated with responsibility and purpose. Ours is a vibrant history boasting a feminine heritage of courage, of flexibility amid change, and of determination. For us, what we think— what we know in our hearts—demands subsequent action. Prayer and performance go hand in hand in a proactive commitment to eliminate injustice and pain in our families.

The topic I have been asked to address is family violence. My assumption is that you, as women of faith, not only wish to recognize and understand it, but also desire to do something about it. Therefore, my challenge to you is to stop abuse in your family today and in society in your lifetime. Five years ago I would have had the initial burden of convincing you there was a problem, especially here in Zion. Today, however, most of you are familiar with an active and horror-filled media and share an honest concern for your LDS community and perhaps even for yourself and your children. Yet, the attitudes of society are still causing us considerable problems.

Violence will not stop in the home until it stops in the mind. Currently the new laws defining child abuse and neglect and spousal abuse are not congruent with our prevailing attitudes toward discipline. Thus, conflicting values result. Parents want to respond to the current value placed on raising re-

Anne L. Horton, assistant professor of social work at Brigham Young University, holds a Ph.D. from the University of Wisconsin and a master of social work degree from George Williams College. She is involved in research and clinical practice in the area of family violence. She has written a book entitled Abuse and Religion: When Praying Isn't Enough. *She has served as a Young Women teacher in her ward.*

sponsible and law-abiding children, yet, at the same time, they are attempting to uphold the "new" belief that corporal punishment is no longer acceptable. The "belt," slapping, or shaking some sense into an errant child are no longer legal alternatives, yet they have not been replaced in most parental repertoires of child-rearing techniques.

Many of you know family violence is common, but do you realize how close it is to you? Have you been a victim personally? In this audience, statistically one in four of you is a *direct* victim.[1] You have been sexually or physically abused by someone—not by your choice. It has made a tremendous impact on your life, and you know who you are. The majority of you, however, are still observers. When you came in, you probably saw yourselves not as directly involved but as an information consumer. Yet, LDS women are all directly involved. As leaders, as teachers, as sisters, we share a common concern, a commitment to provide love and safety in the home.

Let's take a moment to look at this. First of all, the major problem is not *sexual*. Incest and family violence are not expressions of intimacy just because they involve our personal parts and people whom we love. Nor is it just a female concern. For every female victim there is a male perpetrator or abuser who is risking his personal and professional reputation, his family, and his eternal salvation. While it may appear that the victim is most visibly "at risk," the male family member is certainly destined to suffer as well.

Child and spouse abuse are expressions of power, perversion, force, and violence. They are criminal acts. Home is meant to be safe; violence committed there, especially by somebody understood to be a guardian (husband, father, older brother, uncle), is a special betrayal. Someone has physically violated the victims in a way that has destroyed their trust and robbed them of a feeling of personal safety. Fear and shame are constant companions for victims, and this pain, suffering, and feeling of being invaded and robbed of security does not usually go away without help.[2] Thus, all future relationships may be damaged until this trust is restored.

Yet, many of us still want to blame the victim, especially if it's a woman. Why? We want to say she set herself up. She *must* have done something to ask for it. We look at the way a victim was dressed. We want to know what she said or did to place herself in this position.

Why do we do this? We do it because we personally want to feel safe. We want to believe in cause and effect. For if we truly believe battering could happen to anyone, it makes *us* horribly vulnerable. We too have to share the fear that it could happen to us or our children. If we continue to soothe ourselves and say a woman got what was coming to her, if she is guilty of something and we are not, then we believe it won't happen to us. We will be safe. Sisters, this is not the way to protect ourselves.

No child ever *knowingly* (that is, *with knowledge*) asked to be physically harmed or sexually abused. Of course, all of us want to be loved, held, comforted, and fussed over by our family. It feels good to be protected and touched by someone we love. Those are good, natural feelings. And to get those strokes of attention and approval, children will at times do whatever will assure them of acceptance. But no four-, six-, or ten-year-old girl sleeping in her own bed, lying amidst stuffed toys and a frilly quilt, ever invited sexual intercourse with her father or other family members. No young wife, unable to quiet a fussing child, asked to be hit across the face or burned or kicked in the stomach.

In your cul de sac or your block, someone is in pain. We are all at risk. Righteousness is not enough to protect us. Virtue is not being taken away. As victims of physical violence, we are not sinful. We did not "ask for" or cause the abuse. It is the perpetrator who is at fault. Family violence consists of human, physical acts — wrong and painful. Hitting a spouse or child is not acceptable. Beatings are not justifiable. Righteousness has clearly left the heart of the abuser, but the victim did not select the act anymore than did a smallpox victim or arthritis victim or the gunshot victim in a 7-Eleven robbery. Yet many victims of abuse feel responsible. The difference is in our attitude toward this problem. We can't deny that these acts happen just because we don't understand them. Our lack of awareness today is irresponsible and unresponsive to human injustice. Child abuse and wife abuse are not only morally wrong; they are also criminal acts.

Our pioneer women suffered many physical hardships. The difference with incest and beating is that the physical event may have been brief and the physical scars have healed, but the psychological pain continues. Abuse victims need help. Why do we recoil from thinking about this problem? Why do these sisters feel so isolated? So judged? So guilty? Why can't they move on and grow spiritually? Why don't we help them?

The greatest problem today is one of *denial*. We *must* raise our awareness of this issue. Physical and sexual abuse and assault are not rare. They are not a statement about the woman's character. They do not happen only to poor or minority families. In a recent study in Los Angeles and also in a statistical survey regarding child abuse and neglect in LDS families conducted here in Utah Valley, LDS families had a high incidence of these violent crimes — equal to or greater than the incidence in non-LDS families.[3]

In the United States, we have one violent crime every twenty-four seconds, one forcible rape every six minutes. We need to focus on this major problem with our eyes open. For instance, every two hours a woman dies as the direct result of some form of domestic violence. One out of three LDS women has been physically or sexually abused or both. If you aren't the direct victim, statistically someone very close to you is — our women of faith, or approximately one million LDS women.[4]

If you are not or have not been a victim, loved ones and friends who *are* victims need your support and love. They need you to be aware of their struggle to rebuild self-esteem and regain balance in their lives. They need a loving hand and warm heart as they face this challenge, not a cold shoulder. You can be an instrument of healing — a sister in time of need — merciful and loving, not judgmental and unkind.

So today we are at a crossroads, trying to restore law and order, a sense of social discipline, rules and regulations, yet maintain our personal rights as individuals. The focus on individual rights in the sixties and women's rights in the seventies is an acknowledgment that certain forms of inhumanity will no longer be tolerated.

The right to personal safety is a constitutional right not to be confused with feminist values. It has been said that a civilization will be judged by the quality of its mercy. At this point in our civilization, physical and sexual abuse of women and children will no longer be tolerated. We have now made a legal statement. It is time for personal follow-through!

Today, domestic violence is against the law. Yet, acknowledging family violence has not stopped it. We have new rules against it. Practically daily we see bills introduced to tighten the laws — add more years to child abuse sentences, make the penalties stiffer. The problem is not that the laws are too lax; it is that people's attitudes do not truly reflect the law.

How do Americans feel about violence? The economic truth appears to be that they are fascinated by it. Millions of dollars are required to make excessively brutal movies with the expectation of a waiting public audience. Who can deny this high level of social acceptance if so many are willing to pay $4.50 to be entertained by brutality and pain? It truly attracts and repels at the same time. In LDS families, we define abuse on one level, and we define discipline on another. How many of us have hit, slapped, poked, pinched, screamed, thrown car keys, pulled hair, or shoved someone? How many of us have ever been guilty of hitting a bit harder than we intended? How many of us are still doing that today? When we do it, it is defined as "normal"; yet, in others we see the mote more clearly. A recent study of Mormon families revealed that what we do ourselves and see as acceptable behavior and what we would report in others as child abuse were remarkably similar. How narrow the threshold of violence is![5]

Violence is taught. It is passed from one generation to another. To stop child and spouse abuse, we must no longer allow it. Hitting is wrong. Yet, we define abuse differently for different people. Forty years ago, when I was a child, Mr. Sommers, my next-door neighbor, a banker, was known for his temper and was proud of whacking his kids soundly "when they needed it." He was outraged when an officer stopped by to discuss a complaint from a neighbor about his son Richie's stitches. Today, Mr. Sommers would have been arrested. Today, parents must seek new methods of discipline. Hitting hurts; hitting can kill. It is not amusing to threaten to hurt someone. It is not funny when someone says he will kill you or beat you to keep you in line, because some do.

Recently, my daughter reminded Brother White to send his daughter to the sports fireside that evening. "Don't worry," he advised her, "I'll whip her all the way there." I'm sure Brother White meant to be reassuring, but my daughter, truly a believer in nonviolence, said sweetly, "Brother White, you mustn't hit Tanya; even Robbie Bosco isn't reason enough for that!"

Certainly, violence can be explained, but it can no longer be condoned or taken lightly. Attitudes block the spirit of the law, and it is these attitudes that determine what is reported, what is prosecuted, what penalties are exacted.

An important attitude, and one I wish to leave with you, is our notion of what is a woman's issue. I have always been put off by the idea of being linked with the women's movement. *Feminism,* in the LDS community particularly, has so many poor connotations. I have always enjoyed being a woman. I have a dear, though rather sexist, husband and seven pretty terrific children. I fix meals, do not change my own tires or oil (though I know I could), worry about my figure, and am thinking of applying a little Loving Care. Yet, the dilemma before us is one of creating change. Are those of us critically involved in this struggle concerning abuse towards families part of a movement to help victims? Are we part of a movement to stop spouse abuse and family violence?

In my own life, I do not feel repressed or compromised because I know I have a choice. Many women, however, don't know that. For many, alternatives are few. Choices seem non-existent. These victims are afraid to leave and afraid to stay. Some would rather die than face the stigma of abuse—and they may.

I want to remind us all that historically the battered women's movement came out of the women's movement as did the movement against rape. If it had not been for the years of civil rights and antiwar struggles, and if it had not been for the years of struggle by women to articulate the oppression of women in this society, we would still be unaware of such a thing as a battered woman. Women and children would, of course, continue to be beaten and killed. This reevaluation of society was necessary groundwork so that we might change, might articulate that abusive behavior was not individual or aberrant but rather social and political. Cultures, rituals, and customs determine our level of tolerance toward violence. We know in treating violence that the hardest families to reach and change are those that come from cultures supporting wife abuse.

For instance, working with Cuban refugees, I found language barriers, high levels of frustration and stress, unemployment, mental illness, and culture shock; the major obstacle, however, was their inability to understand that it was not right to hit women. In their minds, women were not very valuable, and it was okay to hit them. In the LDS culture, however, women and children have a high social and eternal value. Our Heavenly Father and our Church leaders cherish us and demand our protection. Human rights are a human concern, not a women's issue.

Historically, men have had the legal and social right to control the behavior of their wives and chastise their behavior when appropriate, but appropriate to whom? Although neither the historic nor the legal right of men to treat their wives as property still exists, the social right to beat women is maintained. No analysis of individual pathology or mental illness can adequately explain why millions of women are beaten each year and why this behavior is still socially approved by many. Our religious leaders are spearheading the need to change. President Gordon B. Hinckley, in counsel to priesthood holders, stated: "Perhaps [child abuse] has always been with us but has not received the attention it presently receives. I am glad there is a hue and cry going up against this terrible evil, too much of which is found among our own."[6]

The great American dream of constitutional equality is slow in evolving. What was seen as protective at one time can be defined as oppressive today. (A man's telling his wife to stay home when beasts were roaming the land is considerably different from insisting today that his wife never leave the house.)

At a legal, moral, and social level, we have made a policy statement: no more hitting. Therefore, begin your protest against abuse in your own home. Do you still allow hitting at your house? Do you use physical force yourself? Have you tried to stop it? Today, violence cannot be tolerated in our laws, in our homes, in our minds, or in our attitudes.

An important day came for me five years ago. I sat down with my family and explained to them how I felt. I told them that we must never have any physical abuse—even low level abuse—in our home, no matter what, from that day forward. What that meant on a practical level was that no one would throw a hairbrush in anger or pull the milk carton out of someone else's hands or shove a person in an effort to beat him or her to the bathroom. I also asked them not to raise their voices or have the music at an intense level. Today, at our house, there is no more physical abuse. Even with teenage daughters, hitting is not an option.

If you aren't against violence, you are unwittingly supporting it. Today take an inventory of your attitudes and your behaviors. If you have a problem with abuse at home, that is the place to start. You can be a woman of courage and change. You do have a *choice*, and choosing to *remain* a victim or allowing your children to be victims will have eternal as well as temporal consequences. The Lord has always expected us to do our part. Seek help, and do it immediately. Identify who is at risk, and work toward prevention. Invite specialists to your ward to address this subject directly and explain its dangers and solutions. Send welfare representatives to conferences and training sessions in this area.

Next, be open to your neighbor's pain. Don't close your eyes, but look with sensitivity, new knowledge, and a desire to change, not blame. Investigate treatment options in your community. Offer parenting skills and periodic relief and support to troubled families. An hour or two of your time to an exhausted mother may make the difference between her feeling overwhelmed and alone, as opposed to feeling loved and on top of things again. Do not refuse to look at the problem because it seems too much to take on!

Any Church leader who says he doesn't have any abusive families in his ward is deceiving himself. In research we are often accused of asking only the questions that invite the answers we want. Religious leaders do this as well. Certainly violence in the family has confused the sacred and the secret for too long. Every member of these families is a victim and will pass the pain to a new generation if we do not make responsible changes, ask responsible questions, and offer responsible alternatives.

Be a proactive partner in solving one of the leading problems in this country today. As a teacher, researcher, wife, mother, and LDS woman of faith, I have set a goal to make home a safe place for everyone. If my neighbor is being beaten, I am not safe. Safety is a right in this country, not a privilege, and your attitude plus my attitude will be our assurance for the future.

Today you must stop abuse in your own home, and together we can stop violence in our lifetime.

Notes

1. Murray A. Straus, "Wife-Beating! How Common and Why?" *Victimology* 2 (1977–Winter 1978): 443–58; Diana E. Russell, "The Incidence and Prevalence of Intrafamilial and Extrafamilial Sexual Abuse of Female Children," *Child Abuse and Neglect* 7 (1983): 133–46.
2. Ginny Nicarthy, *Getting Free: A Handbook for Women in Abusive Relationships* (Seattle: Seal Press, 1982).
3. Anne L. Horton, "A Statistical Survey Regarding Child Abuse and Neglect in LDS Families." Prepared as unpublished report, 1985.
4. Marilyn Sherman, "The Economic Roots of Family Violence," *Current Consumer and Lifestudies,* Jan. 1986.

5. Linda Bradley, "A Study of Physical Discipline Practices in Relationship to the Legal Definition of Child Abuse: A Study of 100 Utah Valley Families' Discipline and Reporting Practices," unpublished master of social work research project, Brigham Young University, 1986.
6. In Conference Report, Apr. 1985, p. 66.

INSPIRATION FROM THE PAST

"I rejoice that we can enjoy the privilege of associating together to converse on things of the Kingdom, to comfort and edify each other."

—ELIZABETH ANN WHITNEY

A Legacy *of* Faith

CAROL CORNWALL MADSEN

When Elizabeth Ann Whitney was appointed in 1842 by Emma Smith to be her counselor in the newly organized Female Relief Society of Nauvoo, Elizabeth Ann and the organization she would serve entered the mainstream of an American female religious tradition that had been undergoing dramatic changes for half a century. Since the late 1700s, women had found new avenues of spiritual expression through benevolent associations, like the Relief Society, and had been newly entrusted with custodial responsibility for the prevailing religious and moral values of American society, assignments women came to share with the clergy.

With only a few exceptions, women's participation in American religion, until the nineteenth century, had been largely passive. Following the admonition of the Apostle Paul, women were enjoined to be silent in the churches and were allowed no teaching or ecclesiastical role. Anne Hutchinson, one of the earliest religious nonconformists in American history, was exiled from the Puritan colonies for attempting to assert the preeminence of the biblical teachings of Titus, who exhorted women to instruct one another. Quakerism marked another notable exception, endorsing women's service in the ministry in a prophetic or teaching capacity. But the practice was not acceptable throughout the colonies. When Quakeress Mary Dyer attempted to teach religion in the Puritan towns of New England, she was banished and eventually hanged. Though

Carol Cornwall Madsen received her Ph.D. in American history from the University of Utah. Her dissertation on Emmeline B. Wells was a co-winner of the Mormon History Association's best dissertation award for 1985. She is a senior research historian with the Joseph Fielding Smith Institute for Church History and associate director of the Women's Research Institute, both at Brigham Young University. She has served as the president of her ward Relief Society.

women's religious sentiments were valued and sometimes quoted in Sunday sermons, women as public religious teachers in colonial America were considered heretics.[1]

In 1830 another significant exception to the Pauline decree of silence occurred when the Lord, by revelation to Emma Smith through the Prophet Joseph, as recorded in Doctrine and Covenants 25, empowered her to "expound scriptures, and to exhort the church," according to the spirit that would be given to her. (V. 7.) She was also ordained on that occasion to be "an elect lady," which Joseph Smith later interpreted as meaning "one who presides." When the Relief Society was organized in Nauvoo, Joseph Smith read from that 1830 revelation to Emma "and stated that she was ordain'd at the time the Revelation was given, to expound the scriptures to all; and to teach the female part of the community and that not she alone, but others, [could] attain to the same blessings."[2] Though the privilege was used primarily within the women's organizations of the Church rather than in the general congregation, this practice was a marked departure from traditional concepts of female religious participation.

Like many of her contemporaries, Elizabeth Ann "found" religion during the period of the Second Great Awakening, which swept the New England states and upper New York and moved westward and southward during the early decades of the nineteenth century. Born the day after Christmas in 1800 in Derby, New Haven County, Connecticut, to Gibson and Polly Smith, Elizabeth Ann grew up in a community that had temporarily lost its religious moorings. The Smiths had similarly retreated from orthodox religion, and Elizabeth Ann was reared without religious instruction. She left Connecticut just as the revivalist fervor began to animate the New Haven community, beginning at Yale University, toward a broad spiritual renewal.

Accompanying a well-to-do maiden aunt to the frontier in Ohio when she was eighteen—an unlikely venture for two single women—Elizabeth Ann soon thereafter met Newel K. Whitney, a successful fur trader. In 1822 the two were married, settling in Kirtland, Ohio, where Whitney became a partner with Sidney Gilbert in a successful mercantile business. Naturally religious despite her lack of training, Elizabeth Ann was attracted to the Campbellites, a millennialist sect, which she and her husband joined. Soon disillusioned by the sect's lack of divine authority, the Whitneys sought spiritual help through prayer. One night, experiencing an overwhelming manifestation of the Spirit in which they were enveloped as though in a cloud, they were impressed with the words: "Prepare to receive the word of the Lord, for it is coming."[3] Within months, Parley P. Pratt brought the message of the gospel to the Whitneys. Elizabeth Ann was the first to hear and believe and the first to be baptized.

In her receptivity, her search for spiritual reassurance, and her immediate response to the promptings of the Spirit, Elizabeth Ann followed a pattern that prevailed throughout those days of religious awakening. It was largely a feminine revivalist movement in America; women were converting in greater numbers than men, often leading husbands, family, and female friends into church membership or renewed commitment.[4] No longer content with a silent piety, women sought an active religious role. Their profession of faith engendered a desire for communal religious activity. As one new Protestant convert said:

"I . . . never felt the power of the religion of Jesus until about two years ago. Since that period I have seen things in a new light. I have felt . . . that I am not my own; that my time, my talents, my influence, and my all belong to Him, who has bought me with his own blood. I feel that my life should be a life of active service, and that there is need of my labors in the vineyard of the Lord."[5]

Women's religious enthusiasm found several forms of expression. One was to gather in weekly prayer meetings and special prayer circles to nourish their own newly born faith and to bring other women into the Christian fold. Another was to form religious and benevolent associations, communities of religiously motivated women who wanted to manifest in Christian service their revitalized faith. Throughout New England there developed a profusion of such societies, creating new means of religious participation for women.

The Relief Society came relatively late to this new phenomenon of female religious activity, and for Mormon women, as for their Protestant sisters, it provided a collective religious identity and a sense of empowerment within the ecclesiastical structure of the Church. During 1843, the second year of the Relief Society, counselor Elizabeth Ann Whitney found expanded opportunity for ecclesiastical service, especially in the absence of Emma Smith throughout the season. She conducted the meetings of the society, organized a visiting committee to search out the needy, directed the society's charitable activities, exhorted the members to faithfulness, and served as a model for her Mormon sisters, who found their faith magnified in good works. "I rejoice that we can enjoy the privilege of associating together to converse on things of the Kingdom, to comfort and edify each other," Elizabeth Ann told the Relief Society at a July meeting, and she urged the sisters to "free their minds as the Spirit of the Lord should direct[,] that all should make known the wants of the poor." The minutes reported that the sisters "express'd their minds one by one [and that] a union of sentiment seemed to prevail among them all in forwarding [the work of] the Temple and in relieving the wants of the poor."[6]

The development of religious and charitable associations created a sense of sisterhood among thousands of women nowhere more intensely than among early Mormon women, who not only participated in the great benevolent impulse of the age through the Relief Society but shared the knowledge that they were in the vanguard of the restoration of religious truth.

Another dimension of women's faith expressed itself in the exercise of the charismatic gifts, that is, the demonstration of spiritual power promised to all who believed in Christ. These gifts were encouraged primarily in the millennialist and restorationist sects, which sought a return to the visible manifestations of the spirit of Christ. For Mormons, the Kirtland Temple provided the setting for a latter-day Pentecost, where many witnessed the outpourings of the Spirit, and at the first patriarchal blessing meeting held in the temple, Elizabeth Ann Whitney received the gift of "inspirational singing," as she called it. In a naturally clear and plaintive voice and in the gift of tongues, she sang songs of praise and rejoicing, demonstrating a gift of faith that never left her. "The sweet songstress of Zion," the Prophet Joseph called her, as she comforted him with her singing during the difficult days in Kirtland. A singular blessing given to Elizabeth Ann by Isaac Morley confirmed this special gift: "Thou hast been blest of the Lord by the gift of faith in singing the songs of Zion," he told her. "Thou hast edified and comforted those who have heard. This blessing [of faith] shall be increased in thy bosom by the power and spirit of knowledge."[7] In 1854 Wilford Woodruff wrote in his journal of a visit by Elizabeth Ann Whitney and Eliza R. Snow:

"I read over several of the old sermons of Joseph that were not recorded anywhere except in my journal. We passed a pleasant evening together, and before they left they sang in tongues in the pure language which Adam and Eve spoke in the Garden of Eden. This gift was obtained in the Kirtland Temple through a promise of the Prophet Joseph Smith. He told Sister Whitney if she would rise upon her feet she should have the pure language. She did so, and immediately began to sing in tongues. It was nearer to heavenly music than anything I ever heard."[8]

Not only Elizabeth Ann but many other men and women received and exercised the gifts of the Spirit for the spiritual edification of Church members.

Later on, in Nauvoo, Elizabeth Ann, along with several other women, was also "ordained and set apart under [Joseph's] hand to administer to the sick and comfort the sorrowful."[9] At the same time, he also encouraged women to freely exercise the gifts of the Spirit to uplift, comfort, and bless one another. The sojourn at Winter Quarters seasoned this spiritual power. Together these women of faith met to enjoy what they repeatedly called "spiritual feasts," prophesying, praying, testifying, and blessing one another.[10] Though men as religious leaders were the primary shapers and transmitters of the tenets of faith, through the exercise of spiritual gifts women became vehicles of the Spirit and by this means they too became transmitters of spiritual values and religious faith.[11]

An aspect of the religious experience that captured the enthusiasm of Mormon women was the liturgical or priestly function, represented in temple worship, not commonly available to most religious women in nineteenth-century America. Elizabeth Ann Whitney was the second woman in this dispensation to receive the temple rites, Emma Smith being the first. As a member of what came to be known as the Holy Order, or Endowment Group, Elizabeth Ann and her husband joined a small number of early Saints who received all of the temple ordinances under Joseph Smith's direction before the Nauvoo Temple was completed. One of the significant honors of her life was to give birth in January 1844 to the first child born "heir to the Holy Priesthood and in the New and Everlasting Covenant in this dispensation," a girl whom the Prophet named Mary.[12] When the Nauvoo Temple was completed late in 1845, Elizabeth Ann Whitney, Mary Ann Young, and Vilate Kimball were the first to perform the initiatory rites, repeating the priesthood ordinances for each other and for other Mormon women whom they had previously received in the upper room of Joseph Smith's store as members of the Holy Order. Elizabeth Ann officiated every day thereafter as a "Priestess," a title accorded to all ordained women temple workers in that period. Besides Mary Ann Young and Vilate Kimball, she was joined in this service by Eliza R. Snow, Bathsheba W. Smith, Zina D. H. Young—all future general Relief Society presidents—and several other faithful women, who would continue their work as Priestesses in the Endowment House and the temples of Utah. When Eliza R. Snow preceded many of her sister temple workers to Utah, she sent a poem back to them that suggests the reverence with which they all considered their priestly calling. It ended: "All is well, is well in Zion; Zion is the pure in heart. Come along, ye holy women, And your blessings here impart."[13] Bound together in a network of charismatic and priestly functions, these Mothers in Israel, another designation of spiritual power, created a unique female tradition within the rituals of Mormonism.

Mormon women of the past shared many of the collective religious experiences of their American sisters. On their own initiative women were able to break with the entrenched traditions and create a new spiritual space for themselves. Through organized benevolence, a renewed evocation of spiritual gifts, and, especially for Mormon women, an essential, assigned role in the performance of the saving ordinances of the gospel, women in their various religious settings claimed a vital participatory function. But for Elizabeth Ann Whitney and her Mormon sisters, conversion meant even more than an expanded religious role. For her, she wrote, it meant "a fresh revelation of the Spirit day by day." It meant "a most implicit faith in a divine power," a sustaining faith when one came "unequal to the contest of life's struggles," a "faith in God which has its foundation in the principles of eternal truth."[14]

For these women, who were pioneers not only of a new region but a new religion, the restoration of the gospel opened new avenues of religious participation and laid a foundation of purpose and meaning to their lives which they had not known before. Elizabeth Ann Whitney gratefully embraced every new principle and ordinance of the gospel as Joseph revealed them, amazed that she was among the first chosen to hear the restored message in this last dispensation of time. Her commitment to the principles of truth that she learned from the Prophet Joseph himself remained firm to the end. Of the rich heritage left by our Mormon sisters of the past to the women of the present, perhaps the most significant is their legacy of faith.

Notes
1. Rosemary Ruether and Eleanor McLaughlin, eds., *Women of Spirit: Female Leadership in the Jewish and Christian Traditions* (New York: Simon and Schuster, 1979), pp. 16–17. See also Mary Maples Dunn, "Women of Light," in Carol Ruth Berkin and Mary Beth Norton, eds., *Women of America, a History* (Boston: Houghton Mifflin Co., 1979), pp. 115–33.
2. A Record of the Organization, and Proceedings of the Female Relief Society of Nauvoo, 17 Mar. 1842, LDS Church Archives, Salt Lake City.
3. Edward W. Tullidge, *The Women of Mormondom* (New York: Tullidge & Crandall, 1877), p. 42.

4. Mary P. Ryan, "A Women's Awakening: Evangelical Religion and the Families of Utica, New York, 1800–1840,"*American Quarterly* 30 (Winter 1978): 602–23. See also Keith E. Melder, *Beginnings of Sisterhood: The American Woman's Rights Movement, 1800–1850* (New York: Schocken Books, 1977), pp. 36–43.

5. Melder, *Beginnings of Sisterhood*, p. 36.

6. Minutes of the Female Relief Society of Nauvoo, 15 July 1843.

7. Patriarchal Book B., No. 663, p. 527, in Newel K. Whitney Collection, Box 6, Fd. 25, Archives, Harold B. Lee Library, Brigham Young University, Provo, Utah.

8. Matthias F. Cowley, *Wilford Woodruff: History of His Life and Labors* (Salt Lake City: The Deseret News, 1909), p. 355.

9. "A Leaf from an Autobiography," *Woman's Exponent* 7 (1 Nov. 1878): 83; 7 (15 Nov. 1878): 91. See also 10 (15 Mar. 1882): 153–54.

10. See, for example, Patty Sessions, Diary, 28 Apr., 1 and 28 May 1847, LDS Church Archives, Salt Lake City. See also Eliza R. Snow, Diary, 1 Jan. through 12 June 1847, printed in Nicholas G. Morgan, Sr., ed., *Eliza R. Snow, an Immortal* (Salt Lake City: Nicholas G. Morgan, Sr., Foundation, 1957), pp. 317–24.

11. For a more extensive analysis of this idea, see Ruether and McLaughlin, *Women of Spirit*, pp. 19–23.

12. "A Leaf from an Autobiography," *Woman's Exponent* 7 (15 Feb. 1879): 191; see also 10 (15 Mar. 1882): 153.

13. *Woman's Exponent* 9 (1 Feb. 1881): 131; *Eliza R. Snow, an Immortal*, p. 282.

14. "A Leaf from an Autobiography," *Woman's Exponent* 7 (1 Aug. 1878): 33.

Alice Merrill Horne, Cultural Entrepreneur

HARRIET HORNE ARRINGTON AND
LEONARD J. ARRINGTON

*O*ne of the remarkable women in nineteenth-century Utah was Alice Merrill Horne. Elected to the Utah legislature only two years after statehood, she was one of the few nineteenth-century women to serve in a state assembly anywhere in the nation. In 1899 she wrote and shepherded through the legislature the bill to create the Utah Art Institute, which was intended to "advance the interest of the fine arts, including literature and music, in all their phases within the state of Utah."[1] As enacted, the bill provided for state-sponsored art exhibits and for the acquisition of prize-winning paintings to provide a state-owned collection of art. (The collection was later named after Mrs. Horne, the Alice Art Collection.) Annual exhibits were held in each of Utah's leading cities and at the colleges and universities in the state so they could be widely viewed. The collection, which still exists and continues to be augmented, was the first such state-sponsored collection in the nation. During the 1920s, when the Art Institute was not well

Harriet Horne Arrington holds a B.A. from the University of Utah. She is chair of the women's art exhibits of the Utah chapter of the American Association of University Women. She has taught in the public schools and has served as a Relief Society and Primary president and in various other capacities in the Church organizations.

Leonard J. Arrington received a Ph.D. from the University of North Carolina at Chapel Hill and a D.Litt. from Utah State University. He was the first occupant of the Lemuel Redd Chair of Western History at Brigham Young University, a position he held for fifteen years. From 1972 to 1982 he was also LDS Church Historian and then was appointed director of the Joseph Fielding Smith Institute for Church History at BYU. He has served in numerous Church positions over the years, including counselor in a stake presidency.

funded, Alice decided that if the state was negligent, she herself would exhibit and encourage the public to purchase works of art. She held exhibits in banks, in hotels, and in ZCMI, Salt Lake City's leading department store. Over the next twenty years she sold several hundred paintings and placed at least forty collections of works by Utah artists. Believing that "in each home should hang a good picture," and that "no impressionable child should be denied the privilege of living with one good picture,"[2] she held exhibitions in most of the grade schools and high schools in the state and started permanent collections that still hang in many of Utah's schoolrooms. In this sense Alice has often been referred to as the "First Lady of Utah Arts."

Alice also led crusades to save historic buildings and pioneer landmarks. She was author of two books, *Devotees and Their Shrines: A Handbook of Art* and *Columbus Westward Ho.* The latter is a play in dramatic form used in the public schools. The former work was used for lessons on art appreciation and landscape study by the Church's Relief Societies.

A longtime member of the general board of the Relief Society, Alice wrote some of their first lesson manuals, contributed articles to their magazine, and conducted seminars for local Relief Societies throughout the Mormon West. She was a Utah delegate to the International Congress of Women, held at Berlin, Germany, in 1904 and gave two addresses to that convention. She was instrumental in founding the Daughters of the Utah Pioneers, an organization that now includes more than 22,000 members, and was its first secretary and second president. She was the first woman to be elected chairman of the Democratic Party in Salt Lake County and was historian and state regent of the Utah Chapter of the Daughters of the American Revolution. She was a leading figure in the establishment and operation of "clean milk depots" in Salt Lake City at a time when the provision of pasteurized milk for babies was lacking. Similarly, she organized the Smokeless Fuel Federation and Women's Chamber of Commerce. She was one of a committee of three legislators that sponsored the relocation of the University of Utah to its present site on the hills overlooking Salt Lake City. Finally, in addition to all of this, she was the mother of six children, all of whom, except one who died at age seven months, were achievers and two of whom are still alive. Alice died in Salt Lake City in 1948 at the age of eighty.

The question that naturally occurs is how to account for this woman. She was the product of a plural household — her father had three wives. Were her accomplishments in some way related to her upbringing in a polygamous family? Her grandparents George A. Smith and Bathsheba W. Bigler Smith were pioneer leaders in the Great Basin. George A., an early colonizer, apostle of the Church, Church historian, and a close associate and first counselor of President Brigham Young, was also a leader in the territorial legislature. Bathsheba, a longtime member of the Relief Society General Board and general president of the Relief Society from 1901 to 1910, was also a director of the Deseret Hospital Association and matron of the Salt Lake Temple. So the government of the Church and Territory was part and parcel of Alice's home life. Was it, therefore, the advantage of family connection that propelled her forward? Her husband, a Salt Lake banker who adored her, was complaisant and supportive; should much of the credit for her accomplishments be given to him? The values that prompted her to participate so vigorously in many of these activities were tenaciously held by her church, The Church of Jesus Christ of Latter-day Saints. Was it, therefore, her Mormonness that inspired her leadership? Where does one go for an explanation?

Although a good case could be made for each of these hypotheses, any single explanation would be simplistic. Obviously, her family, her teachers, her community, and her church each influenced her. More important, during the time she was growing up, there was close congruence between family, church, schools, and community. Brigham Young was president of the LDS Church, to which the vast majority of Utah's residents belonged (perhaps as high as 98 percent when Alice was born); he was also governor of the territory (part of the time de jure, part de facto); and, following his oft-expressed objective, all pioneer life was — or aimed to be — a seamless web. Politics, economics, education, recreation, worship, charity, and even art were aspects of religion, of church concern, and of ecclesiastical leadership. Everyone was expected to be engaged in building the kingdom of God; that is, in working toward commonly understood group goals. When the Saints first arrived in the Great Basin, Brigham declared:

"You are commencing anew. . . . Build cities, adorn your habitations, make gardens, orchards, and vineyards, and render the earth so pleasant that when you look upon your labours you may do so with pleasure, and that angels may delight to come and visit your beautiful locations. . . . Your work is to beautify the face of the earth, until it shall become like the garden of Eden."[3]

Although it was important to settle as many communities as possible, immigrate as many converts as possible, and improve the level of living to the point that each family could enjoy a competence, the primary goal of their society, Young believed, should be the improvement of people by the nurture and maintenance of educational and cultural organizations. The Great Basin, he said, "is a good place to make [Latter-day] Saints."[4] The Latter-day Saints "have been taken from the coal pits, from the iron-works, from the streets, from the kitchens and from the barns and factories and from hard service in the countries where they formerly lived." They belonged to "the poorest of the poor."[5] "Here [in our mountain retreat] we can cultivate every science and art calculated to enlarge the mind, invigorate the body, cheer the heart, and ennoble the soul."[6] In contradistinction to the society in which he grew up, here children and young people were encouraged to dance, to study music, to read novels, "and do anything else that will tend to expand their frames, add fire to their spirits, improve their minds, and make them feel free and untrammeled in body and mind. . . . Every sweet musical sound that can be made belongs to the Saints and is for the Saints. Every flower, shrub, and tree to beautify, and to gratify the taste and smell, and every sensation that gives to man joy and felicity are for the Saints who receive them from the Most High."[7]

By the time Alice was in secondary school—that is, by 1880—a whole generation had been reared under the principles of cooperation, mutual sharing, earth improvement, social improvement, and mind improvement that Young and his associates had promoted. Survival in their hospitable environment came first, perhaps, but afterwards came beautification, learning, and wholesome recreation. In any event, it was the obligation of each individual to contribute his or her labor, talents, and genius to building the kingdom—that is, to improve society.

These values were emphasized at the so-called University of Deseret, the Church-run school that Alice attended as a teenager during the 1880s. Many of her classmates also achieved largely, and one must surely attribute much of their activity to the training and encouragement they received from the University faculty. Just how did that training impinge upon Alice Merrill Horne?

Alice Merrill was born in a log cabin on January 2, 1868, at Fillmore, Utah, the daughter of Clarence Merrill and Bathsheba Smith. (Fillmore is about 150 miles south of Salt Lake City. Because of its central location it was, for a period, the capital of Utah.) She was the third daughter and fourth child in a family of fourteen children. Shortly before Alice's birth, reportedly at the urging of her grandfather, George A. Smith, her father married additionally Julia Felshaw, a widow nine years older than he, by whom he had a son nine months after Alice was born and a daughter two years later. When Alice was eleven he also married Isabelle ("Belle") Harris, a very bright and spunky girl of eighteen, by whom he had two sons. Clarence was divorced by Belle four years later, when Alice was fifteen.

Because of these plural-family arrangements, Alice's father was not an ever-present dominating figure in her mother's home, although he apparently preferred to stay with Bathsheba as much as he could. Alice and her thirteen full brothers and sisters were given household and family responsibilities at an early age. She first went to school at the age of six, but it was a ward school, run by the bishop and whoever he could get to be the teacher (apparently Delilah Olsen), and operated three or four months each winter. Alice said she had pleasant memories of being whisked through the snow by sled to the little rock schoolhouse. The students had "nice home-made seats and desks, good maps, blackboards," and there was a village library.[8]

That much of her training was in her mother's home was not necessarily a disadvantage. Her mother was full of energy and good humor, took an active part in ward plays, of which there was a constant succession, composed and recited humorous poems and songs, and assured an active social life for the family. A Utah pioneer of 1852, Alice's father was intelligent and had a pleasant personality. He ran Fillmore's telegraph office, taught school, directed the ward theatricals, and always had some income from various enterprises that he managed. His first plural wife, Julia Felshaw, had a dressmaking and hatmaking business in Fillmore. In 1876 Clarence bought a farm in Marysvale, some thirty-five miles south of Fillmore, and Alice and her siblings spent some of their summers there. In 1877, when Alice was nine, her mother also moved to Marysvale, where Clarence taught at the local school. The next year Clarence was elected superintendent of schools for Piute County. After that year, because of a drouth, he moved to Richfield, in Sevier County, where he managed the local cooperative general store. After four years there, in 1883 the family moved to Salt Lake City for Bathsheba and her children to be near her mother and for several of the children, including Julia's, who later moved to Salt Lake City, to attend the city's schools. They remained there until 1892, after which Clarence and some of the family returned to Fillmore.

When Alice was seven, her maternal grandfather, George A. Smith, died, leaving her grandmother, Bathsheba W. B. Smith, alone. The grandmother, who had lived briefly in Fillmore and had often visited with the Merrill family, invited one or more of the Merrill girls to live with her in Salt Lake City. Alice went to live with her the next year on a more or less permanent basis, although she returned to live with the Merrills each summer.

Because George A. Smith had been a member of the First Presidency of the Church and Church historian, Bathsheba's gable-roofed home was located on Brigham Street (now South Temple Street), just east of Main Street and across the street south from the Lion House and President's Office of Brigham Young. Upon Alice's arrival in Salt Lake City, therefore, her grandmother promptly took the eight-year-old across the street to Brigham Young's office, introduced Alice to him, and according to her daughter, Brigham charged Alice "to make her grandmother's happiness her first duty and to grow up and try to be like her."⁹ Bathsheba and Alice were often present for Brigham Young's daily "family home evenings," at least until his death in 1877, and thus Alice, for a year at least, had a chance to be a member of Young's large extended family. (Young's family met each evening after dinner in the Lion House parlor and had family prayer, after which they played games, put on skits, played musical instruments and sang, and otherwise enjoyed being together.)

Like most women in nineteenth-century America, Grandmother Bathsheba had little formal education, but she was intelligent, aware, and interested in events, both local and national. Her home enveloped Alice in what she called an "Arabian Nights atmosphere." There were many original paintings, colorful quilts and coverlets, lace curtains, blinds with hand-painted scenes. Her library included a variety of magazines and newspapers. The youthful Alice devoured *Century, Godey's Lady's Book, Scribner's, Youth's Companion, Leslie's Illustrated News Magazine, Chamber's Encyclopedia,* and other national publications, as well as such local publications as *The Juvenile Instructor, The Woman's Exponent,* and the *Deseret News Weekly.* Bathsheba had studied painting in Nauvoo, Illinois, when the Mormons were located there, and had painted portraits of both Joseph Smith and Brigham Young, as well as such genre scenes as fruit, landscapes, and children. She gave instruction to Alice and kindled an interest in art that remained with Alice throughout her life. Grandmother Bathsheba was also active in the Relief Society — she was a member of the "inner circle" that eventually became the general board of the Relief Society and later served as general president of the Relief Society of the Church. Thus, important women in the territory were often in Bathsheba's home—women influential in politics, ecclesiastical affairs, civic affairs, literature, education, and the visual, literary, and performing arts. Country girl that she was, Alice profited from this exposure during her growing-up years.

One of the inducements offered by Bathsheba to have Alice Merrill stay with her each winter was that she would see to it that the girl attended a good school. Perhaps the best in the territory was the Thirteenth Ward School, which was the school of the ward in which Bathsheba's home was located. We have no record of Alice's progress in that school until 1879, when she turned eleven. Under the leadership of John R. Park, president of the University of Deseret, the Thirteenth Ward School was incorporated as a training school, and existing records show Alice Merrill enrolled as a fourth-grade student during the school year 1879–80, with Orson Howard as a teacher. The twenty-seven-year-old Howard was a native of Mill Creek, Salt Lake County, had studied at the University of Deseret during the four preceding years, and was now principal of the Thirteenth Ward School. The year after this class, Howard went on to Grinnell College in Iowa and came back to the University of Deseret as a professor of natural science and English literature, and was one of Alice's instructors during her "college" years. The extent of personal instruction Alice had in the fourth-grade class is indicated by the fact that there were only seven students in the room—three in the fourth grade, two in the second, and two in the first grade.

Alice, who on the school records is often listed simply as "Allee Merrill," remembers: "We chose up sides, took opposite ends of the room, and vied in distinct rendition of alternative voices from 'Woodman, Spare That Tree,' 'The Bells,' and 'Excelsior.' The old walls would fairly ring as we recited those grand old poems."[10]

Alice continued studies in the training school again in 1880 and 1881. Then in 1882, when she was fourteen, she enrolled for more advanced study, in what we would call today secondary education, but which was then the principal offering of the University of Deseret, a school with approximately 200 students. During her first year Alice studied grammar, arithmetic, orthography and punctuation, elocution, writing, reading, and geography. During her next year, 1884–85, she and five others were considered prepared to enroll in college or college preparatory courses. They took ancient, medieval, and modern history; physiology and hygiene; botany and zoology; rhetoric and English literature; and astronomy. During her second year of "college" she had courses in Chaucer and Shakespeare, history of civilization, physics, civil government, writing, freehand drawing and vocal music, and "normal," which was presumably a course in the theory and practice of teaching.

There is no record of Alice's being enrolled for the school year 1886–87; perhaps she was a student teacher in a grade school class. But we do know that she was associated with the University in extracurricular ways. She organized a Shakespeare Society, with fifteen young men and fifteen young women, who met regularly to study, memorize, and produce Shakespearean plays. She also participated in a choral group of persons of her age. And she organized in 1885 the Friendship Circle, consisting originally of six persons—three girls and three boys, who met each Saturday in her grandmother's parlor and discussed a variety of religious, cultural, political, and social topics. The group soon expanded to thirty, and after the members were married it was converted into a women's club; it continued to meet throughout Alice's lifetime.

With fifteen others from the University, Alice graduated in the class of 1887 and was asked to read the valedictory essay at the commencement exercises. Appropriately, her essay was entitled "Lady Macbeth and Ophelia."

There is no question that the University engaged in what today would be called "consciousness raising." We do not have Alice's essay at her graduation, but we do have the commencement talk four years later by Mary Elizabeth ("Mamie") Woolley. Among other things, Miss Woolley said:

"The young ladies of this institution stand on an equal plane with the young men and receive from them the respect which equals demand. Sex with us is no distinction. If there is anything to be performed and a lady is capable, the fact of her being 'fair' does not deter her. Her opinion is expressed and sanctioned, her testimony borne and sustained the same as that of her brethren."[11]

This attitude, inculcated in Alice, remained with her throughout her life. An exemplification of this female assertiveness was told to us by LeConte Stewart, a ninety-six-year-old Utah artist whose paintings are currently going through a popular and critical revival.[12] In 1916, having established a certain reputation as an artist, LeConte, then twenty-five, was called by the Church on a mission to paint murals for the Hawaii Temple. Knowing he would be there for at least two years, he invited his Utah sweetheart, Zipporah Layton, to go to Hawaii and marry him. Her bishop, however, said that was against all the rules; men on missions were not allowed to marry. Alice, who had exhibited and sold some of LeConte's first paintings, heard of this denial and promptly "marched" into the office of the president of the Church, Joseph F. Smith, and asked him to override the bishop. President Smith said, "You know very well I can't do that; I must enforce the rules." Alice, according to the account, "wagged her finger under his nose," and said, "Now, Joseph, I don't care what the rules are. You are the president, and you can bend the rules if you want to. You are going to allow Sister Layton to join Elder Stewart in Hawaii so they can marry." Taken aback by her assertiveness, President Smith meekly replied, "Well, Alice, if you insist!" In a few days, Zipporah was on her way to Hawaii, and she and LeConte began a marriage that lasted sixty-seven years. As this incident illustrates, Alice did not hesitate to use the force of her personality to get things done when the occasion was important enough to require it.

During her senior year, according to family remembrance, Alice was courted by three University students who were also associated with her in the Shakespeare Society. Two of them went on to law school at the University of Michigan, and she wrote to them for a period. But she finally decided to marry a young man four years older than she, who had gone to work for Utah State National Bank in Salt Lake and eventually became the bank's cashier. George Henry Horne, son of a plural family and also a loyal Mormon, had been in Alice's Shakespearean Club, in the same vocal group, and in the same Friendship Circle. Alice later said she was glad she had married him because he was so supportive of her — in looking after the household, in contributing to various causes in which she engaged, in driving her around the state in his car, and in giving her encouragement in her ecclesiastical, political, and cultural activities. He was, in short, a "modern" husband, which leads us to wonder if women's assertiveness of the 1880s produced other husbands of this disposition.

No doubt, part of the motivation for Alice's subsequent activities was the superintendence of the University by Dr. John R. Park. A native of Tiffin, Ohio, and possessor of an M.D. degree from New York University and Bellevue Hospital, Park had spent a winter as a teacher in the Salt Lake Valley, converted to Mormonism, and served five years as principal of the ward school in South Willow Creek (now Draper). Under his energetic and enlightened leadership, the South Willow Creek school soon gained a reputation as the best in the territory. Because of the training they received from Park, many young persons of promise began to make their mark in educational and professional circles in the territory. When Brigham Young and his associates decided to "refound" the University of Deseret in 1869, Park was appointed its president.

Starting from no campus, no faculty, no library, no museums, no lecture rooms, and no students, Park soon had the best of all these among the colleges in Utah and produced persons of eminence in many professions. Alice Merrill, who was often in his home because her sister married his housekeeper's son (Park was a bachelor), profited from close association with him and his faculty for many years. Indeed, she was one of Park's closest advisers, just as he was one of hers.

Alice enjoyed the daily assemblies of students and faculty at which there was a reading of the Bible and of various literary masterpieces, prayer by a student, brief talk by Dr. Park, short talk by another faculty , and then dismissal to class. Among her teachers — persons who also were close associates throughout her life — were the following:

1. Park, who taught her the theory and practice of teaching, arithmetic, grammar, and spelling and punctuation.[13]

2. Joseph B. Toronto, son of Giuseppe Toronto, native of Sardinia, and Eleanor Jones, native of Wales, both early converts to Mormonism. Toronto had been a student at the University of Deseret from 1869 to 1875 and was regarded as a near genius in mathematics and ancient languages. He entered West Point in 1875 but resigned to accept an appointment at Deseret as instructor in ancient languages and history. He served there until 1889. Toronto taught Alice the history of civilization; ancient, medieval, and modern history; and bookkeeping.[14]

3. Joseph T. Kingsbury, a product of Utah schools and self-effort, was born near Uinta, Weber County, in 1853, but lived most of his youth in Salt Lake City, as did Alice Merrill. He studied at the University of Deseret from 1872 to 1875 and then attended Cornell for two years, studying the physical sciences. He went to the University of Deseret in 1878 and taught Alice physics, chemistry, geology, civil government, and geography. He was later president of the University of Utah from 1897 to 1916 and was also a close friend of Alice.[15]

4. Orson Howard, her fourth-grade teacher who had since received a degree from a midwestern university, taught Alice zoology, physiology, botany, astronomy, rhetoric and history of the English language, English literature, and Chaucer and Shakespeare.[16]

5. Joshua H. Paul, born in Salt Lake City in 1863, had graduated from the University in 1879 with certificates in normal and natural science. He taught Alice writing, reading, grammar, and geography. He went on to become president of Brigham Young College in Logan from 1891 to 1894 and in 1894 became president of Utah State Agricultural College (now Utah State University). He later returned to the now University of Utah as professor of nature study. He and Alice worked together on several projects involving conservation and beautification.[17]

6. Evan Stephens, a Welsh convert to Mormonism, eventually became director of the Mormon Tabernacle Choir. He taught Alice vocal music and worked with her in the Junior Tabernacle Choir, in several operatic productions, and in other musical capacities.[18]

7. George M. Ottinger, a Mormon convert from Pennsylvania and an enthusiastic Utah artist, taught Alice freehand drawing and painting. Quite possibly Ottinger had more influence on Alice than any other teacher—at least it was he who reinforced her interest in art, already implanted by her grandmother Bathsheba in her more formative years. Born in Pennsylvania, Ottinger had begun to paint when he was nine. When the aunt and uncle who cared for him died, he lived for a time with friends and relatives until the age of seventeen, when he decided to go to sea. He circumnavigated the globe on a whaler, joined the California Gold Rush, took passage to China, put in at Honolulu, and then decided in 1853 to return to New York City to paint. He studied under Robert W. Weir of the Hudson River School and at the Pennsylvania Academy of Fine Arts in Philadelphia. There he converted to Mormonism. He went to Utah in 1861, arriving just as the Salt Lake Theatre was about to open. He was engaged for four years painting scenery for the theater. Later he worked as a phototinter, established an art gallery, and did some painting. He was a teacher at the University of Deseret in the 1880s and helped Alice to create the Utah Art Institute.[19]

After her graduation, Alice taught at the Washington School in Salt Lake City. She married George Henry Horne early in 1890 and gave birth to a daughter by the end of the year. In 1894 George was called to serve as a proselyting missionary for the Church in the Southern states. He remained two years. Meanwhile, Alice went back to teaching school in order to support herself, her daughter, and her husband on his mission. During the same period she continued to study art, this time under J. T. Harwood, Mary Teasdel, and John Hafen, all prominent Utah artists. Her second child was born the year after her husband's return from his mission.

Two years later Alice was nominated by the Democratic Party for the legislature and was elected for a two-year term. Thus began the personal career that caused her to be a leader in Utah's Democratic Party, in the Relief Society, in Utah art circles, and in many other community affairs. Those who knew her have testified of her creative leadership, her courage in tackling unfriendly persons and unpopular issues, and her contagious enthusiasm. She was also a lover of the beautiful and thought the kingdom the Latter-day Saints were building ought to be beautified with lovely art and architecture and with beautiful people. In tracing her life we have interviewed literally dozens of older artists who say that she was the one person who, through her sponsorship of exhibits and ardent promotion of their work, made it possible for them to earn money on their paintings through the 1920s and 1930s. They have testified that she was truly the first lady of Utah art. Clearly, Professor Ottinger and others at the University, together with other religious and family influences, had inspired her to devote her life to what she regarded as the development and appreciation of the good and the beautiful.

In an age in which individualism is spreading, social relations are atomizing, religious life is increasingly privatized, and the customary pattern of livelihood is for each individual to seek to maximize his or her personal income regardless of social consequences, it is nostalgic to contemplate Alice Merrill Horne, the exemplification of community spirit, a builder of social institutions, an advocate of using public resources to enhance public culture. The product of a commonwealth that emphasized collectivity, unity, order, and nationality, she labored for community good and encouraged in selfless ways the organic improvement of the cultural and social life of Utah.

Sources and References

Alice Merrill Horne wrote extensively about her life and intended to publish a personal history, but she died before that goal was realized. As the oldest living grandchild of Alice, Harriet had the opportunity of typing portions of that history.

Over the years, we have also interviewed all of Alice's living children, many of her grandchildren, one brother, one sister, nieces and nephews, and several persons who were close friends and associates of Alice. We have obtained transcripts of the courses she took at the University of Deseret from the Records Office of the University of Utah. We have also gone through newspapers, magazines, art publications, legislative journals, and other printed sources. Much material is at the Utah State Historical Society, University of Utah, LDS Church Library and Archives, Daughters of the Utah Pioneers Library, and Brigham Young University Archives. We have an extensive file on Alice, her life, her achievements, her writings, and her works of art, but we have cited only those sources that are particularly pertinent to this paper. We hope that a full-scale biography will be forthcoming.

General Utah histories include Richard D. Poll, ed., *Utah's History* (Provo: Brigham Young University Press, 1978); and S. George Ellsworth, *The New Utah's Heritage* (Salt Lake City: Peregrine Smith Books, 1985).

Mormon histories include James B. Allen and Glen M. Leonard, *The Story of the Latter-day Saints* (Salt Lake City: Deseret Book, 1976); and Leonard J. Arrington and Davis Bitton, *The Mormon Experience: A History of the Latter-day Saints* (New York: Alfred A. Knopf, 1979). Brigham Young's life and influence are treated in Leonard J. Arrington, *Brigham Young: American Moses* (New York: Alfred A. Knopf, 1985). The University of Deseret, which was converted into the University of Utah in 1892, is treated in Ralph V. Chamberlin, *The University of Utah: A History of Its First Hundred Years, 1850 to 1950* (Salt Lake City: University of Utah Press, 1960).

Brief biographies of Alice Merrill Horne can be found in: Robert S. Olpin, *Dictionary of Utah Art* (Salt Lake City: Salt Lake Art Center, 1980), pp. 126–28; Zorah H. Jeppson, "A Brief Biography of Alice Merrill Horne by Her Daughter," typescript in possession of the writers; Raye Price, "Utah's Leading Ladies of the Arts," *Utah Historical Quarterly* 38 (Winter 1970): 65–85; Jill C. Mulvay, "Three Mormon Women in the Cultural Arts," *Sunstone* 1 (Spring 1976): 29–39; Leah D. Widtsoe, "The Story of a Gifted Lady," *Relief Society Magazine* 32 (Mar. 1945): 150–55.

Notes

1. *Laws of Utah,* chap. 29, "The State Institute of Art, Approved March 9, 1899."
2. Alice Merrill Horne, "Utah Art," *Young Women's Journal,* 20 (Dec. 1909): 602.
3. *Journal of Discourses,* 26 vols. (Liverpool, 1854–80), 8:79, 80, 83; 1:345.
4. *Journal of Discourses,* 4:32.
5. *Journal of Discourses,* 6:70; 10:358–59; 13:61; 14:38.
6. Manuscript History of Brigham Young, LDS Church Archives, Salt Lake City, 23 Aug. 1848, p. 57.
7. *Journal of Discourses,* 9:244.
8. Daughters of Utah Pioneers of Millard County, *Milestones of Millard* (Fillmore, Utah, 1936), p. 35.
9. Zorah H. Jeppson, letter to Dr. Vern G. Swanson, 2 Oct. 1984, copy in possession of the writers.
10. Alice Merrill Horne, "Child of the Frontier," pp. 8–9, microfilm of typescript in possession of the writers. "Woodman," by G. P. Morris, 1830; "Bells" by Edgar Allan Poe, 1849; and "Excelsior" by Longfellow, 1841.
11. Farel C. Kimball, ed., *Mary E. Woolley Chamberlain: Handmaiden of the Lord* (Salt Lake City: Privately Printed, 1981), p. 99.
12. See, for example, Wallace Stegner, "The Power of Homely Detail," *American Heritage* 36 (Aug./Sept. 1985): 62–69.
13. On Park. see Ralph V. Chamberlin, *Memories of John Rockey Park* (Salt Lake City: The Emeritus Club, 1949).
14. See Chamberlin, *University of Utah,* p. 593.
15. Chamberlin, p. 212.
16. Chamberlin, p. 587.
17. Andrew Jenson, *Latter-day Saints' Biographical Encyclopedia* (4 vols., Salt Lake City, 1901–36), 1:619.
18. Jenson, 1:740; 4:247.
19. Chamberlin, *University of Utah,* p. 590.

WOMEN IN
AN INTERNATIONAL CHURCH

Each culture has great gifts to bring to Church membership. . . . Let us not forget that people are always more important than programs. Let us be willing to learn from those we would teach.

—BETTY VENTURA

Cultural Differences and Gospel Unity

BETTY VENTURA

*A*s an introduction to my remarks on cultural differences in the Church, I think it would be interesting to note how present-day membership is distributed among the nations of the world. Currently, what are the ten main languages spoken in the Church? After English, the next two most frequently spoken languages are Spanish and Portuguese. And then, of the next seven languages, two are the languages of Europe, German and French, but the other five are languages spoken in the Orient and the islands of the Pacific: Japanese, Korean, Chinese, Samoan, and Tongan. The European nations, once the wellspring of members for the Restored Church, today hold less than 2 percent of Church membership. It is in Mexico, South and Central America, and the exotic lands across the Pacific where thousands are joining and missions and stakes are being organized.

These figures are given to point up our need to recognize cultural differences and to resolve them, both as a Church and as individual members. Sensitive to this problem, the Translation Department recently evaluated the Church curriculum materials. I was named coordinator for the group, but the real team of cultural experts who analyzed curriculum materials was the native translators from the different areas of the Church: Polynesians, Japanese, Koreans, Chileans, Mexicans, Guate-

Betty Ventura holds a B.A. from the University of Utah and has done graduate foreign language studies at the University of Mexico and Brigham Young University. She served a mission to Mexico and has served as a Relief Society president in the Spain Barcelona Mission and as a Spanish-language temple worker at the Swiss Temple. In her work with the Translation Department of the LDS Church, Sister Ventura reviewed the Catalan edition of the Book of Mormon and supervised its printing. She has served as Relief Society president in the Salt Lake Park Cambodian Branch. She and her husband are the parents of four children.

malans, and so forth. They were the ones who read through the manuals or sat through the filmstrips and then jotted down what to them was relevant and gospel and what was simply American or Wasatch Front culture and would not be understandable or might be counterproductive with their people.

As the manuals and audiovisual productions passed through our hands, the list of cultural differences grew longer and longer. We came to realize how very complex this subject is. There were varying degrees of irrelevancy and inappropriateness. There were illustrative anecdotes that taught the wrong message, and even some pictures and line drawings that were offensive. Yes, the subject of cultural differences is complex, and I hope I do not oversimplify as I try to categorize these cultural differences under three very broad headings.

First, there are some very deep-seated differences in customs and traditions between societies. In this category I would place most of the problems that plague Church curriculum writers of youth manuals: the differences in dating and courtship customs, the practice of openly discussing morality in the classroom or in video presentations, the contrast between the independence enjoyed by our American youth and the parental control found in other cultures, traditional attitudes about obedience and respect for parental counsel. These are major differences, distinguishing whole societies. How can a single set of manuals be written to serve them all? Does one water down the admonitions and the danger signals for youth in one society, or put ideas into the heads of young people in another? Does one focus a lesson on wise decision making, when in some cultures it is the parents who will make those same decisions and obedience to parental counsel is more valued than youth's choice of action? In order to accommodate cultural differences, we tend to word lessons in broader and broader generalities, until we find we have sacrificed much of the effect that our instruction should have.

Perhaps the overall solution to this problem is to produce regional versions of our manuals and programs, targeted specifically to the differing needs and cultural contexts of the major regions of the Church. If our instruction could thereby be culturally specific, it would likely be more effective for specific audiences.

The second category of differences I would describe as controllable cultural barriers. These differences are those little signs of Americana that unwittingly creep into Church materials, perpetuating our image as an American church—not the international, universal church we claim to be, but an American church universally translated. These American symbols appear in many forms: in audiovisuals as English text and in youth manuals as football games and campouts, social clubs and school dances—American youth on a seemingly perpetual vacation. Sometimes the elements are the American flag, community action, free elections, and other democratic processes that, unfortunately, do not exist worldwide. Sometimes the barriers are the translator's problem: crossword puzzles, jingles, the play on words, devices we Americans use to spice up our lessons to entertain students.

One of the most persistent marks of the American church is the affluence that inadvertently becomes a part of audiovisual materials: spacious homes and yards, wall-to-wall carpeting and built-in kitchen cabinets, big cars and imposing chapels. Perhaps those who have served foreign missions have had the experience of showing a new Church film to local members. Seated there in the darkened room and seeing the film for the first time, the missionary was momentarily back home again and was deeply touched by its message. But when the lights were turned up, the audience commented: "What big cars they have in America!" "What luxurious chapels!" "Did you see the wood paneling and the stone fireplace?" Somewhere, amid distracting background details, the plush furniture and modern kitchen appliances, a message has been lost, or the wrong message conveyed.

A multitude of cultural differences could be cited under the heading of Americana. But most of these I categorize as controllable. We, the preparers of the materials, can learn to recognize and then eliminate, or at least control, these distracting elements. We can and must learn to speak in universal

141

terms and to use modest or neutral visual settings as we teach and preach the message of the restored gospel worldwide.

The third area, I think, affects us most as lay members of the Church. This area of cultural differences pertains only indirectly to curriculum and audiovisual and written presentation, but it presents an enormous challenge to each of us as individuals. I would call this the area of human relations, or more precisely, of humanizing relations. It consists of many qualities and customs, all of them interpersonal, interacting relationships between ourselves and those of other nationalities.

This third area surfaced and crystallized as native translators were asked about the cultural differences they saw between the United States and their homelands. What was hardest for them to grow accustomed to in our society? What customs did they miss most from their own? I would like to describe some of these customs as they have been described to me.

First, I found that many foreign cultures have a truly marvelous concept of the extended family. As various translators pointed out, they don't need lengthy lessons on the importance of looking out for Grandma or visiting the lonely maiden aunt. In their cultures the extended family—cousins, uncles, great-aunts, and so forth—*is* the immediate family. The Tongan says: "In our islands even your sixth or seventh cousin is your brother or your sister; you treat him or her as you would the closest member of your family." In all of these Polynesian lands there are no rest homes, no old folks homes. "Even if an elderly person is not anyone's grandfather, there is a place for him in someone's home, to be clothed, fed, and cared for until he dies. Parents take care of their children when they are small, and the parents are sure that these same children will take care of them when they are elderly."[1]

In the Cambodian culture, family members are also protective. Children when very young learn the responsibility of looking after each other. In the Cambodian branch I attend, brothers and sisters at first almost panic when they are separated into different Primary classes. There is one little boy who week after week escapes his teacher to sit outside his little sister's classroom, waiting for her. The eight-year-old carries the three-year-old in his arms. Children have been taught from their earliest years to look out for each other.

Latin American children learn to share when very young. The South American says, "You do not eat in front of a person who has nothing. You share, no matter how little you have."[2] This they have learned from watching parents who open up their homes — whether to the relative or to the stranger, whether for one meal, or for one night or many nights. They learn by example that no matter how small or humble the home, it is to be shared with the visitor.

Latin Americans have other great humanizing qualities. We Americans sometimes grow impatient with what we feel is their utter disregard for punctuality. "Mañana, siempre mañana," we say. Do we realize that there is a basic difference in values between our two cultures? To the Mexican and the South American, *people* are most important, not programs or schedules. How people feel about each other and how they express those feelings have precedence over time frames or deadlines. There is a slower pace with the Latin, a taking out of time to show warmth, to express feelings — the little personal joke, the inquiry about another's family, the caring. That is the Latin American's way of running his timetable.

A great quality of the Polynesian peoples is their attitude of respect towards their leaders. When a leader says to do something, it becomes scripture. "Get a haircut." "Wear a white shirt when you pass the sacrament." In the words of a Tongan translator, "Some people call this kind of obedience blind faith, but I call it faith believing,"[3] — accepting the leader's word.

From time to time Korean and Japanese translators have come into the Translation Department in Salt Lake for training sessions. As they quietly enter our department, we Americans suddenly become the ones receiving the training. We find ourselves talking softer, working longer and harder, and even being more courteous to each other. Sometimes we greet each other with the short bow, so typical with the Orientals. Among their many other gifts, these people bring dedicated effort and a quiet courtesy to our boisterous and informal office life.

One further example from the Cambodians. These humble refugee people come to us shod in sandals and wearing light-weight tropical clothing. They come straight from refugee camps, stripped of material possessions, some even without photographs of the dear ones left behind. Once here they begin the slow process of learning impossible English, of surmounting their own personal series of cultural barriers, hoping as quickly as possible to enter the lowest level of the American labor market.

Sopha Rin, her husband, and three small children live in a tiny two-bedroom apartment in west Salt Lake. There are two things hanging on their front room wall. One is a large poster of the Christus. The other is a small missionary card written in Cambodian and English, giving the four steps to prayer. This year Sopha's family of five was joined by an aunt and her two daughters. These three women had lived for five years in a refugee camp in Thailand until they were sponsored by Sopha and her husband. (To be a sponsor doesn't mean one has money; it means one has a heart and is willing to look after a refugee family until they can get their feet on the ground.)

That little apartment was already crowded with old couches and beds. And now eight people share the space, three newly arrived refugee women in one bedroom, and Sopha's family of five in the other, until next month when Sopha's baby comes and they will be six.

This in broad lines is a third area of cultural differences in the Church. The first two are curriculum oriented, to be solved in their own way. But this third area and its resolving are our own, yours and mine. How do we stand against the measuring stick these foreign cultures bring into our lives? Each culture has great gifts to bring to Church membership. We Americans have our gifts: we know how to organize and systematize, how to harness computers and have them serve the Lord's work, how to prepare and print attractive teaching materials, and distribute the gospel message throughout the world. But let us in all humility look at these other cultures, not at their dirt floors or sandaled feet or humble downcast expressions, and recognize the great gifts of compassion, love, and caring they bring to us. Let us not forget that people are always more important than programs. Let us be willing to learn from these we would teach. Are these their gifts not "lovely," "of good report," and "praiseworthy," and should we not "seek after" them? (Articles of Faith 1:13.) Some of these newer cultures in the Church may appear unconventional to us, and we react to their seemingly strange dress and impossible languages. But we may someday find that in the Lord's timetable these peoples were placed after us in hearing the gospel message because they have less to learn.

Faced with all of these cultural differences, how do we achieve gospel unity? There are no easy answers, for it is a mosaic we want to achieve, not a melting pot. This we can know for sure: things are going to get harder before they get easier. As missionaries cross the thresholds into the African or Arab world, into Islamic, Buddhist, Hindu, and other non-Christian societies, we will be meeting new and greater cultural challenges. And we will need to have resolved the old ones, if we are going to be successful in gaining and retaining membership in those exotic lands. In curriculum planning we will learn to become more discerning between what is gospel and what is no more than clinging to our American way of thinking. Those who prepare Church teaching materials will pass through refining fires as they discover what intrinsic, basic gospel principles really are. Perhaps some day new hymns will be written, using strange new tone structures, to be accompanied by zither or drum. And Church congregations, sitting side by side on mats or rugs, will sway and clap rhythmically together as they sing the songs of Zion.

I have a feeling that for lay members like ourselves, a true gospel unity must come about not through curriculum changes but on an individual basis. This is the path. Each of us first enlarges his or her own personal vision through reading "out of the best books" and becoming "acquainted with languages, tongues and peoples." (D&C 88:118; 90:15.) Then we extend outwards, beyond the academics and the book learning, thirsting to interrelate with peoples of other cultures. It may come in our own home ward or through a second mission, as we rub shoulders with new ethnic groups and learn to love them, understand their needs, and serve them. They may be Spanish-speaking or Vietnamese, Cambodian, or Nigerian.

One step in this pathway, our individual quest, will be to analyze the importance of material possessions in our lives and just how we are spending our mortal probations. Sometimes bridges need to be built, but sometimes we Americans just need to restructure our own end of the bridge. Then each of us will be able to cross over that bridge, in a spirit of unconditional love, to where the teacher both teaches and learns, and the learner unknowingly teaches the teacher much more. And of course, in that climate of teachability and unconditional love, there *will* be unity. For "light cleaveth unto light" and spirit speaks to spirit, overcoming all linguistic and cultural barriers. (D&C 88:40.) And we shall someday find that perfect unity and oneness in the family of our Heavenly Father, for by then we shall have realized that if we are not one, we are not His.

Notes
1. Tekehu Munanui, Tahitian translator.
2. Elizabeth Smania, Spanish translator.
3. Tangata Niumeitolu, Tongan translator.

Third-World Heidis

VAL D. MACMURRAY

I am honored to address you today on the topic of cultural differences and gospel unity. As executive director of the Thrasher Research Fund, most of my professional activity has to do with administering pediatric research grants that seek to improve the health of infants and children in third-world countries. My work takes me to research and demonstration projects in South America, Central America, Mexico, Asia, and Africa. They have not failed to impress me — indeed, they would impress anyone — with the desperate need mothers in those countries feel to make the world better and safer for their children.

I'd like to phrase those needs — and some of the opportunities the Church offers the world's children — in terms of my oldest daughter, Heidi, who in a few years may well sit in such a group as you but who celebrated her seventeenth birthday in March 1986.

Heidi is lucky to be born in the United States for many reasons, not the least of which is that being born female did not automatically jeopardize her survival. In many developing countries, girls receive less nutrition as babies. Girl babies are less likely to be taken to the hospital when they are ill, and they seldom receive equivalent education. These discrepancies last their entire lives. According to the International Labour Organization's current report, "Women are one-half the

Val D. MacMurray is executive director of the Thrasher Research Fund (an international health organization), associate clinical professor in the Department of Family and Community Medicine at the University of Utah, and adjunct professor in the MHA/MBA Graduate School of Management at Brigham Young University. He taught previously at Tufts University and at the University of Calgary. He has served as assistant commissioner of LDS Social Services and as manager of research and staff development for the Welfare Department of the Church. He received his Ph.D. degree from Boston University.

world's population, one-third of the official labour force and do nearly two-thirds of the world's workhours. They receive directly only one-tenth of the world's income and own less than one-hundredth of the world's property."[1]

Heidi has two brothers and two sisters. If she had been born in Africa, she would probably have eight or nine siblings; and at least one, perhaps two or three, would have died in infancy of diarrhea or infection. Fifty thousand children die *every day* in the third world because of diarrhea alone.[2] At least that many more are disabled because of disease, malnutrition, and lack of sanitation and health facilities. I think the only time Heidi has not had access to a flush toilet has been on mountain climbing expeditions, an interest she is developing with considerable skill, or in national parks where sanitary and fully equipped privies are usually available. She has never been hungry in her life for more than a few minutes unless she has been voluntarily fasting. In many places in Africa, if she had survived infancy, the chances of receiving adequate nourishment as a child and as a young woman are only fifty-fifty.[3] Ten million children annually are stricken by nutritional blindness; half a million of them will be blind for the rest of their lives, even though enough vitamin A to protect a child for a year costs only four cents.[4]

Heidi has never drunk contaminated water in her life. If she lived in an African city, she would have only a 50 percent chance of having dependable access to reasonably safe and clean water. In thirty-eight countries in rural areas, fully 91 percent of the people lack ready access to clean water. They often have to walk between five and ten kilometers and then have to carry the water home in basins or jerry cans.[5]

If Heidi were to become ill, our family has literally hundreds of physicians and specialists to consult and the resources of several large, well-equipped and well-staffed local hospitals. When her children are born, she can assume that she will have competent obstetrical care. The developed countries of the Western world average one doctor per 300 to 700 people. In contrast, some countries in Africa have 35,000 to 45,000 people per doctor with the numbers soaring to double or triple that number per pharmacist. Even midwives average about 1 per 5,000.[6]

Although there is a statistical possibility—less than 1 percent—that Heidi may die in childbirth, it is highly improbable. Maternal death rates in developed countries are 3 to 30 per 100,000 live births. In contrast, in most developing countries, the death rate is often more than 500 per 100,000 live births. In some parts of Africa, over a thousand of every hundred thousand women die in giving birth.[7]

Nor is death the only hazard involved with pregnancy. In the developing world, women receive significantly fewer calories and much less protein than they need when they are pregnant and nursing. If Heidi were in Africa, there is a 50 percent chance she would be anemic. If she were pregnant, the chances would rise to 66 percent.[8] Her children would probably be spaced eighteen months apart. Exhausted from fieldwork and lacking sufficient food, both she and the child would suffer. There would not be enough milk for the baby and, back in the fields soon after the birth, she might unintentionally malnourish her child because she is too tired to walk back and forth from fields to home to breastfeed it four or five times a day.

Her children would be frequently ill—up to 75 percent of the time, adding to her emotional and physical burdens in caring for them. Ten percent of the family income would go into seeking medical care, but she would routinely have to wait in a clinic three hours to see a health worker who very likely would not have the proper equipment and medicine to help her child.[9] And that's not counting the time it would take to walk to the clinic and back again, carrying the child.

Although all too many American teenage women become pregnant unintentionally and out of wedlock, Heidi has received instruction about her own anatomy and sexual functioning. As her parents, we anticipate that Heidi, for both religious and practical reasons, will have healthy, wanted children. Over 50 percent of the girls in developing countries bear their first child while they are still teenagers. Experts have estimated that if these women could become mothers later, perhaps 30 percent more of the firstborn children would survive.[10] Children born less than two years apart have about a 50 percent higher risk of dying in infancy or childhood.[11]

As parents who seek to develop a healthy, loving relationship with each other, we want the same for Heidi and her future husband. With the view of marriage as a union of full partners, it is distressing to us that several thousand girls in Africa are married before they are fourteen and usually have six or seven children by the time they are twenty-five. Many women do not survive. Nor do their children.

Heidi has already had eleven years of school. She plans to attend college as a matter of course and will probably choose a major in the humanities since she excels at drama, art, and music, and enjoys literature. She has been in public schools for all of her education; but if she had been in Nigeria, the African country I have visited most frequently, public schooling would have been available to her for a maximum of only six years. Even then, only 42 percent of the children actually attend. Literacy runs between 25 and 30 percent in that nation. In developing nations as a whole, only six of ten children enroll in elementary school. Only three of the six will reach fourth grade, and only one will go as far as secondary school. In the field of education, being born female is a definite disadvantage. Twice as many boys as girls receive education in third-world countries.[12]

As an American teenager, Heidi has tremendous vitality and energy. As a child, she had the usual childhood illnesses, like measles and chicken pox. A vaccine for measles has already been developed that will protect her children. A vaccine for chicken pox is expected within a few years. She caught scarlet fever; but even so, none of her ailments were life threatening. What is more serious for Heidi is a chronic neurological condition that has developed within the last eight years. This condition is easy to control with medication, and Heidi leads an entirely normal life. But if she were in a third-world country, the medication would not be available, and she would suffer debilitating seizures. Also, she would have had only a 20 percent chance of receiving the 50 cents worth of vaccine that would have protected her against measles, tetanus, polio, pertussis, diphtheria, and tuberculosis. Malnutrition and infectious diseases work together in a deadly partnership to kill children. During the seasonal famines in Nigeria, measles can kill one child in four. During the Nigerian civil war, the death rate from measles doubled.[13]

Heidi can look forward to a life expectancy of about seventy-eight years. As her parents, Maryann and I look forward to at least thirty-five more years. In Africa, if I followed the national statistics where life expectancy is forty-nine, both Maryann and I would be dead within five years.[14]

As Heidi explores her future, she can choose from a multitude of professions and jobs that will utilize her tremendous ability to deal skillfully with people. She enjoys her work as a teacher's aide at a grade school as part of a released-time program through her own high school and also her work at ZCMI department store as a clerk on a schedule that varies between ten and twenty hours a week, depending on the season. She has access to a family car for her own transportation to and from these jobs and earns enough at $3.60 an hour to keep her car fueled, buy some of her own clothes, and pay for much of her recreation outside the family.

If she lived in Nigeria, the chances are 65 percent that she would be a farm laborer, working the fields with almost no tools, with few fertilizers or insecticides, and without access to hybrid seed. She would be doing between 70 and 80 percent of the work in the fields and producing 40 to 50 percent of the food, then preparing food for the men, feeding the children, cleaning, fetching firewood and water, and caring for the elderly and sick. The per capita income in that nation in 1982 was $860.[15]

The implication of my comments is that Heidi is a pampered princess, privileged to survive and thrive while millions of children die or suffer from lessened productivity all their lives because of where they were born. From one perspective, this is true; however, we think not in terms of privileges but in terms of responsibility. Maryann and I hope we are teaching Heidi and her brothers and sisters that they have both the opportunity and the responsibility to use those advantages to assist in what her generation will view as great strides in improving life in the third world.

Even though literacy is only 50 percent at best, that is still up from 30 percent thirty years ago. Although 44 percent of the third world's women were illiterate in 1980 (709 million), the percentage is predicted to drop to 27.6 by the year 2000. However, that will then be 1 billion, 123 million women. The current life expectancy of forty-nine years is actually an increase of twelve.

Dr. William Foege, former director of the Centers for Disease Control and president of the American Public Health Association, reported at Thrasher's annual meeting in April 1985:

"For many years, I used to say that a child born in the third world today had a better life expectancy and a lower risk of infant mortality than my grandmother did when she was born a century ago in Europe. It crept up on me over the years that that was no longer true. It is now possible to say that a child born in most third-world countries today has a better life expectancy and a lower risk infant mortality than my *mother* did when she was born at the beginning of this century in the United States. And now it is actually true that there are some children born in third-world countries that have a better life expectancy than *I* did when I was born."

He continued with some encouraging statistics: in Colombia in 1984, immunization jumped from 40 to 60 percent because the country organized to protect its children through three special immunization days.

Thanks to the World Health Organization, about 50 percent of the children in third-world countries have had some contact with immunization programs, if only a single dose of vaccine.

The PanAmerican Health Organization has set the goal of eradicating polio from this hemisphere by 1990, and Rotary International has offered to supply all the polio vaccine any third-world country can use for the next twenty years, a $120 million commitment.

Smallpox was eradicated from the globe in 1979.[16] October 26 each year marks another anniversary of the reporting of the last case of that deadly disease. I firmly believe that malaria, which currently afflicts more than 200 million people, will be eradicated in my lifetime.

What role can the Church play? What difference does being LDS make in the lives of third-world women? Let me just share a couple of vignettes with you. One is of Mary Ellen Edmunds, associate director of training at the Missionary Training Center near the BYU campus in Provo. Last year she was project director of a Thrasher-funded group teaching basic nutrition, sanitation, and water purification to families in Eket, Cross River State, Nigeria. Mary Ellen is a small woman, but she has a continent-sized heart. I've felt a lump rise into my throat as I've heard her tell about sitting in a Church meeting, holding a seven-year-old who weighed twenty-three pounds. You may know that the average American five-year-old weighs about forty pounds. She helped teach a family how to treat their children for worms; one of those little children was so ill from worm infestation that she thought he would die. She was gone from Nigeria for about three months, and when she returned, he *ran* to meet her. She had never seen him run before. He had never had the energy.

One of the women in that project is named Helen Bassey. Ann Laemmlen, the project director, commented after visiting Helen: "She looked like a million—hot, tired, dirty, and with only a wrap around her. Her head was uncovered, and she had obviously been working very hard. She was very happy to see me and laughed her Helen laugh as she told me she had been working *very* hard ever since morning. I asked, 'What have you been doing?' She laughed and took my hand and led me to one of the three rooms that made up their cooking area. Unbolting the door, she led me inside, and the sight left me speechless! The room had been thoroughly cleaned out, and all around us were dishes—clean, clean dishes! All morning long she had been working very hard to clean probably every dish she owns. It was in yesterday's workshop that we learned how to properly sanitize dishes. I was so thrilled I . . . hugged her and we laughed together, and she squealed in delight at how happy and surprised I was. She was *so* proud. She told me she had washed everything in hot soapy water and let everything drain dry in the sun. There on a sheet of zinc sat basins and plastic baskets and trays full of sparkling clean dishes. On the floor on the other side of the room were all of her pots and pans, from large to small, clean and shiny. All of them were covered by two pieces of blue plastic tarp, also cleaned. I doubt whether that room has ever seen anything like this in the history of its existence!"[17]

One of the other women in the project is Cecilia Dickson Paul. In her late twenties, she has five living children; three others have died. Her husband is a farmer and handyman. Cecilia is different because she has had eight years of schooling, even though circumstances prevent her from using her education professionally. Her background, however, is making a significant difference in her family. Her hunger for knowledge made her the first in line to learn more about keeping her children healthy, and she has embraced the gospel, rejoicing in its outpouring of knowledge. Ann told of visiting Cecilia on the same day and seeing her pride at having been able to purify her drinking water and having up-to-date records on the children who were receiving treatment for worms.

Cecilia has a daughter who is about Heidi's age. Already, because of Cecilia's values and the gospel, Violet's life is different from that of other Nigerian girls her age. Her parents have shielded her from proposals of marriage that would curtail her education and future economic contributions to her family. They have urged her to plan for her future, to prepare herself with the tools and skills of an educated person to make a difference to her people. I think of the difference that the gospel has already made to Cecilia, how the Church becomes a pipeline not only to the restored truths of the gospel but to the secular truths of conquering disease, malnutrition, and poverty. Violet will live a different life from that of Cecilia because of the Church. Cecilia's grandchildren will also have different lives.

I hope that one of the reasons for that difference will be you. Sitting in this room, I am convinced, are women of compassion, vision, and, above all, competence, who will find ways to solve the problems of sharing information and resources across national boundaries, of communicating facts of life and death to women who are used to being ignored or hushed. Many of you either have served missions or will, bringing the gospel vision of women as cherished daughters of our Father in Heaven and as responsible cocreators of life. Whether you marry or not, you can nurture and enhance life for the world's children. And I hope for Heidi that she is among your number.

Notes

1. Cited by Nancy Fyson, "A Woman's Place," *CWDE Cartoonsheet 14: Women and Development* (London: Centre for World Development Education, 1983).
2. Dr. Inyambo Nyumbu, "Water Supply and Sanitation," *World Health: The Magazine of the World Health Organization,* Aug.–Sept. 1985, p. 27.
3. Shushum Bhatia, "Status and Survival," *World Health: The Magazine of the World Health Organization,* Apr. 1985, p. 13.
4. "Vitamin A Saves Sight!" *World Health: The Magazine of the World Health Organization,* Nov. 1985, p. 17.
5. Dr. Fawzia H. Aboo-Baker, "Culture and Tradition," *World Health: The Magazine of the World Health Organization,* Aug–Sept. 1985, p. 20.
6. Alexander B. Morrison, "Perspectives on International Health: Are We Our Brother's Keeper?" Paper delivered at the first annual meeting of Collegium Aesculapium, Provo, Utah, July 1983, p. 5. Photocopy in my possession.
7. Deborah Maine, "Mothers in Peril: The Heavy Toll of Needless Deaths," *People* 12, no. 2 (1985): 6–8.
8. S. Hamilton, B. M. Popkin, and D. Spicer, "Maternal Nutrition Problems in Developing Countries," in Christopher Roessel and Michael Favin, eds., *Maternal Nutrition: Information for Action Resource Guide* (Geneva, Switzerland: World Federation of Public Health Associates, 1983), p. 2.
9. "Organizing Health Delivery," *CARE Briefs on Development Issues,* no. 4 [n.d.], p. 6.
10. "Short-Changed!" *World Health: The Magazine of the World Health Organization,* Apr. 1985, p. 18; "Facts about Fertility," *People* 12, no. 3 (1985): 2.
11. John Hobcroft, "Survey Throws New Light on Key Policy Issues," *People* 12, no. 3 (1985): 4.
12. Rebecca Cook, "Progress toward Equality," *People* 12, no. 2 (1985): 4.
13. Dr. L. A. Arevshatian, "African Immunization Year, 1986," *World Health: The Magazine of the World Health Organization,* Aug.–Sept. 1985,

pp. 22–23; Dr. Mesfin Demisse, "Drought and Famine," *World Health: The Magazine of the World Health Organization,* Aug.–Sept. 1985, p. 25.

14. Patricia W. Blair, "Health Challenges in the Developing World," *CARE Briefs on Development Issues,* no. 4 [n.d.], p. 2.

15. "Western Africa," *The World Bank Annual Report, 1984* (Washington, D.C.: The World Bank, 1984), p. 84. Estimates for 1982 in U.S. dollars.

16. William O. Foege, address to the Thrasher Research Fund Annual Meeting, 15 Apr. 1985. Transcript in my possession.

17. Report to Thrasher Fund Executive Committee, 21 Feb. 1985, Thrasher files, Salt Lake City, Utah.

Behavioral Differences Are Like Language Differences; or, "Oh Say, What Is Truth?" vs. "Do As I'm Doing"

JOHN P. HAWKINS

*A*s we seek to become a worldwide church, we must increasingly understand the character of culture and of cultural differences, and we must consider carefully the bearing these have on the way we approach Church administrative procedures and customary Mormon ways of doing things. To help us understand an approach to culture and the nature of Church procedures, let me first give an example of the kinds of problems we face. Then I will tease out a definition of culture and an approach to behavior that will help us understand the episode I described. Finally, I will discuss the implications of the definition of culture and the approach to behavior for general Church process in the light of the LDS Church's goal of becoming a world church. This process will enable us to reflect on the question: what impact do cultural differences have on achieving a unity of the faith?

Mormon Life in Small-Town Guatemala

Some years ago, my wife, Carol Lee, and I spent two years in a small town in western Guatemala. Our task was to discover and understand the social life and culture of the people of the

John P. Hawkins received his Ph.D. from the University of Chicago and is associate professor of anthropology at Brigham Young University. Formerly coordinator of Latin American studies in the Center for International and Area Studies at BYU, Professor Hawkins conducted three years of on-site research on family and church in Guatemala and Mexico. He and his family have also lived in Germany while researching the role of family and group dynamics in the United States Army. His Church callings have included bishop and stake high councilor.

community, most of whom were Catholic. We attended our own Mormon services as we went about learning the nature of Catholic belief and practice. What we saw—the behavior system of the Mormons—was just about what one would expect to see in the United States, though on a smaller scale. The church building, for example, was small, but it too had a chapel, classrooms, piano, a kitchen with stove, oven, and refrigerator, and an outdoor basketball court. Attendance was modest—forty on a medium Sunday, sixty on a well-attended Sunday, thirty on a poorly attended Sunday. The ward records suggested that some four hundred Mormons had membership in the unit, but who they were and where they were were not always known. The same Sunday services were held as in the United States: priesthood meeting, Relief Society, Primary, Sunday School, and later sacrament meeting. On Tuesday nights the youth of the Church went to the chapel in the evening for Mutual activities. The local members expressed a warm testimony of the gospel. Most of them were good, faithful people, absolutely willing to do exactly what the gospel required of them. Indeed, most of them were willing to make any sacrifice, and many had given up friends and reduced their family associations and ties as part of the cost of joining the Church. Missionary work was slow, however, and the missionaries complained that the people of both the Spanish town and the Indian town were hard-hearted and unreceptive. While the Church was not exactly thriving, the members there were proud of their little ward and, indeed, had good reason to be proud.

As I learned more and more about the daily lives of the ordinary non-Mormon people, I slowly came to understand what they thought of the active Mormons in their midst. Our Guatemalan Mormons, it turned out, had a bit of a scandalous reputation. Two of the Mormon teenage women, I was told, were known to be unmarried mistresses of non-Mormon males in the community. Another young Mormon woman was reported to be having an affair with the elders and was famous for having sustained this activity for some years. Bear in mind that the active branch was small and that this reputation applied to three out of only four or five young women in the ward.

In one form or another, our Catholic friends let us know they thought it was awful that the Mormons had so little concern for the reputation and morals of their young women. And they let us know that they themselves would not listen to the Mormon missionaries precisely because of the Mormon lack of concern for the morality of their youth. On the other hand, the missionaries thought they were being rejected because of the influence of Satan in hardening the hearts of the people against them.

The contrast between what the Mormons were trying to accomplish among themselves and what the non-Mormons thought of them could not have been more stark. What caused such opposing views?

When we interviewed the Mormons, we found a house of faith and a house of trust — trust in the leadership of the Church and in the revealed basis of the Church's programs. The manuals said to have a youth program and to hold it on a weekday evening. The North American missionaries who assisted the ward and advised the branch and ward leaders over the years had seen Mutual organized and implemented that way in the central stakes of the Church. Because the youth program was for the young and because the limited number of faithful adults was involved in staffing priesthood, Relief Society, and other ward leadership positions, the youth program was left to the single youth to staff and operate. They did a good job. The activities included dances in the ward building, games, and lessons. Who came? The single youth, of course, and the missionaries and their investigators. That was the procedure followed since the foundation of the branch, when the missionaries had complete charge and the program was being inculcated, until the time we were there, when the system had been turned over to the faithful local people. The North American mission presidents who visited the branch and even the native stake president who visited the ward approved. After all, the native stake president had been to general conference and had visited wards on the Wasatch Front. He knew how things were supposed to be, and the Guatemalans wanted to do it right. They were not about to be second-class citizens in the Church by running a program that deviated from the revealed procedures of their Salt Lake Valley example. So do it right they did. As a result, the cultural gulf, the differences in custom between these Guatemalan Saints and their Utah leaders was being reduced.

At the same time, the cultural gulf between these Guatemalan Saints and their non-Mormon Guatemalan neighbors was widening. Some of the Church procedures looked a little strange to the rest of the non-Mormon community and had done so even to these Mormons when they had been investigating. Yet these Mormons had testimonies and were willing to do anything to bring themselves closer to a gospel life. They gave up liquor. The men gave up adulterous relationships. They learned to read the scriptures. They enjoyed improved family lives in many cases and had numerous other confirmations that what they were about was a worthwhile change in their way of life. This was the material result of following God's principles as brought to them by the priesthood and organizational leadership of the Church. As a result of obeying these commandments, their lives were healthier, happier, and spiritually more satisfying. All of these things came to them through the program of the Church, so they were determined to follow the program. One needed to follow the prophets, and here in faraway Guatemala, the prophets spoke through their representatives, the missionaries, and through the manuals. If the program manuals and customary procedure of the Church said youth meetings were to be on a weekday evening, that is when they were held. The youth would go to the ward house on Tuesday evenings for their activities. The adults would not. After all, these were Mormon youth, committed to the values of the gospel, and there was no need to chaperone them as much as was needed among the non-Mormons. The members knew they were to become a separate and peculiar people. So, a separate and peculiar people they became. Let me tell you why and how they became peculiar, more peculiar than the leadership ever would have desired.

Why did much of this Mormon behavior look strange and peculiar to the non-Mormons? Non-Mormons interpreted the faithfully imported Mormon behavior within the Guatemalan symbolic dictionary and premises with which all Guatemalans were raised. Let me be specific. The present-day culture and society of Guatemala are the result of a colonial history. A primary goal of the colonial system was to establish control over others and to extract services from those below one in status. That goal continues to be sought. Since the beginning of the Spanish colony, men have been expected to seek control over others and especially over women. Indeed, men are expected to seek sexual favors from women. Moreover, women are expected to do the bidding of men. Since the families of each class and ethnic level want to maintain their own blood purity and must exercise control over their own domains, and since women are considered weak and susceptible to the wiles of men, any self-respecting family must necessarily chaperone very carefully its unmarried daughters. Obviously, any self-respecting man must constrain the behavior of his wife and suspect sexual overtures from other men toward his wife and daughters. Therefore, young, unmarried women, especially, and women of childbearing age, generally, must always be chaperoned and kept very close to the home or, ideally, kept within the house. Parents who do not keep their daughters chaperoned adequately are, in effect, inviting men to approach them for sexual favors. Since women are taught from a tender age to accede to the wishes of men, they will very likely succumb. Therefore, according to Guatemalan societal norms, those who do not chaperone their daughters closely must not care a whit about their daughters' morals or the family's reputation in the community.

This cultural logic was, of course, used to interpret the behavior of all in the community, including the Mormons. Since Mormons did not chaperone their daughters at youth activities—neither in the evening walk to the chapel, nor at the chapel, nor during the night walk home—Mormons must be a loose and immoral people. Mormon parents, for reasons the non-Mormons could not comprehend, obviously did not care about their children. This being the case, non-Mormons felt free to ask Mormon girls for a night out. The problem developed from the fact that if the young Mormon girls were asked enough, their earlier socialization to serve the wishes of men triumphed over the teachings of the gospel. This was the case for two of the girls, who were indeed sexually involved with non-Mormon men.

The third girl's reputation was besmirched for more subtle reasons. For numerous reasons, many people in Guatemala choose not to enter legal marriages sanctioned by either the state or the Catholic Church. The result is that socially acceptable common-law unions are publicly proclaimed and condoned by parents when they allow a young man to cross the threshold and take up residence in the house of their unmarried daughter. In the case of the Mormons, the missionaries had wanted a place to live, and the parents, being poor but faithful and trusting the missionaries, gave the missionaries residence even though an unmarried daughter still lived in the home. That was not too bad, for the non-Mormon people knew that Protestants allowed their ministry to marry. But there were always two of them — that was strange; and they kept changing every two or three months — that was appalling. In the minds of some, surely the wild tales of Mormon polygamy must be true if they allowed their ministers to behave like this!

Of course the missionary work went slowly! Could the Spirit really bear witness to the truthfulness of the message from a group whose behavior was saying that they did not care about the morals of their children?

Theory

What are the implications of this tale? They can be explained only in terms of a careful understanding of the nature of behavior and the definition of culture.

I define culture as a system of fundamental premises about the nature of the world and the human beings that populate it. These premises are lodged in the minds of the participants of the society. The premises are not explicit. Indeed, it is very difficult for the participants of the system to become aware of their own premises. But the premises drive their behavior. That is the deepest and most subtle aspect of the cross-cultural

162

problem. Differences in premises between cultural systems are the most tricky to deal with, and I have not analyzed culture at this level.

Rather, I have focused on the level of customary behavior. I define behavior as any bodily movement. What is interesting to me as an anthropologist is patterned, or customary, bodily movement, precisely because any patterned bodily movement is likely to be meaningful. In other words, customs are meaningful: they send messages. Moreover, since customs send messages, they cannot be erased or substituted for other customs without changing the entire message system. One of the goals of the anthropologist is to discover the meanings of behavior. In the process, the goal is to come to understand — to read — the messages being communicated in the behavior. Remember, for example, that in Guatemalan society crossing the threshold means marriage. (It is a bit more complicated than that, but the implications are still the same.) Remember that being unchaperoned means having no moral values, whereas being chaperoned represents appropriate behavior. Patterned behavior almost always has meaning attached by contrast with other possible behavior patterns in the same situation, which would have other meanings. Behavior is a form of language and has a dictionary of alternatives: a certain performance has a meaning, and its nonperformance may well be an antonym. That is the case in every society. The dictionary of behavior cannot be altered; it is a framework within which one must live. Behavior is meaningful, just as spoken language is meaningful. Indeed, spoken language is a form of behavior. It is movement of the mouth, mouth behavior — that is, verbal behavior that has meaning.

What we most often forget, however, is that both verbal behavior and bodily behavior are almost entirely arbitrary. The arbitrariness is easy to see in verbal behavior. If I want to convey the meaning of "I go to town" to someone speaking Spanish, I will say, "Voy al pueblo." Everyone knows that "I go" and "voy" are arbitrary but patterned mouth movements intended to convey a meaning and that to convey the same meaning in the two meaning systems requires different behavior. In one meaning system you mouth-move "I go" if you intend to get the meaning across. In the other you mouth-move "voy." The same with "town" and "pueblo." Arbitrary mouth movements are behavior. Sometimes one can get amusing correspondences between closely similar mouth movements that have totally different meanings when used. For example, the mouth movement behavior of *embarrassed* in English is sufficiently similar to the mouth movement of *embarasada* (pregnant) that it causes no end of jollity when naive missionaries speak to local Latin Americans.

Precisely the same thing happens with other kinds of bodily movement. Each has a meaning. To an American, walking to the chapel unchaperoned means something like, "Her parents trust her; she is independent." But to a Latin American, it says something closer to, "Her parents do not care at all about her morals, and neither does she." We would not want our Latin American brothers and sisters to say such a thing in verbal behavior. It is neither the doctrine nor the intent of the Church to be or to appear to be immoral. Why do we allow them to say it in their bodily behavior?

The answer, I think, lies in a problem in our own American cultural system from which the leadership draws its deepest cultural roots. Culture, you will recall, is the system of fundamental premises by which the world and its people are interpreted and evaluated. In American culture, success is defined in terms of accomplishment, and accomplishment is measured in behavioral terms. In the Mormon-American culture, specifically, success is measured in behavioral terms called "activity." Through time we have come to establish a proper mode of doing all sorts of religious things and to codify these procedures in the handbooks. We then count the amount of this standardized activity for both the individual and the institution anywhere in the world.

That works quite well in one meaning system. But when we export worldwide the precise behavioral procedures needed to measure activity to another meaning system, the behavior, as we saw, may take on quite unexpected and unfortunate meanings to persons who are outside the increasingly unified world Mormon cultural-behavioral system. That is the problem.

The solution is to treat religious behavior exactly like language. Everyone in the Mormon Church leadership recognizes that we must move our mouths in a different pattern of behavior if we are to use language to communicate in the United States and in Latin America. We do not use Utah or American English to transmit our message when in Latin America or in China. Similarly, we must be prepared to behave in a particular way in Latin America, or anywhere else, differently than we do in the United States if we visitors or the local members are to communicate the same message. We as leaders and custodians of the institution that brings the gospel become uncomfortable, though, when we contemplate change in sacrament meeting or in the time or manner of the customary performance of other Church procedures. Yet, if we are unwilling to tolerate a considerable amount of behavioral variation in the procedures, the inevitable result will be that the customary procedures set up in Utah will force the local people of the foreign regions to convey an untruthful message to both the members and the surrounding community.

Let me use a linguistic analogy for what will happen if we become locked in a set of behavioral procedures and fail to recognize that behavioral procedures have arbitrary and differing meanings in each society. Suppose we want to convey the meaning of the scriptures around the world. But suppose we felt that chanting them in English was the only proper thing to do. Upon going to Guatemala, we would then have to teach the members to chant in English, and if they were to learn the meanings in the scriptures, they must in essence learn English. But if they learn English and speak in English, no one from the outside community will be able to learn the message till he or she learns English. That would absolutely isolate the converts. They would become an English-speaking religious enclave in Guatemala, unable to be understood by the rest of the Guatemalans. Indeed, they would become a peculiar people.

Similarly, when the behavioral procedures that work well because they communicate well in one meaning system are used to try to communicate in another meaning system, the result will be incomprehension, misinformation, and rejection by the non-Mormon local people. There will arise an inevitable tension because the faithful local people must chafe against the conflicts between the imported procedures and their own culture. To reduce the conflicts, the local members have two choices. On the one hand, they may drop out of the Church and melt back into the parent culture of the country. The result, from the Church's standpoint, is a great deal of inactivity. On the other hand, they may choose to isolate themselves from their parent culture and immerse themselves wholly in the new Mormon way of life, behaving as much as possible as a Utah or United States Mormon would. If they do that, they become better connected and increasingly similar to their worldwide Mormon community that is behaviorally communicating in the Utah-American variant of United States culture. But at the same time, they become isolated from and odd-looking to the non-Mormon men and women they would try to convert. That is precisely what happened in applying the North American approach to the youth program in Guatemala. The Guatemalan converts became one with their North American brothers and sisters in the procedural faith. They were pleased to find the improvements of the gospel in their lives, but they were taught to do it in a way that isolated them from proper communication with their countrymen," and they, thereby, violated the missionary premise of the Church. Adherence to a worldwide standardized form of behavior leads to failed communication, oddity, unacceptability, and isolation of the emerging Mormon convert community vis-à-vis their countrymen. Such isolation is both necessary and acceptable when it is induced by obedience to the basic commandments. But it is both unnecessary and counterproductive when it is based on obedience to the procedures and customs of the Church as it has developed in the Western United States.

Is there a possible solution? I believe there is, but in order to implement it, we must remember that the goal of the Church is to communicate a true message to those around us rather than to make the traveling world leaders culturally comfortable and assure them that they are indeed in the same Mormon church wherever they go. The purpose of behavior is to communicate. The first step, then, is to decide what needs to be communicated, what is the truth that is to be conveyed to others through our behavior. For example, we might decide that what we want to say in the Guatemalan community (or any other, for it is the truth) is that "Youth are important," and that "Mormons stand for personal morality and social development." To say this effectively in the Guatemalan behavioral language, we would decide to hold both youth meetings and Relief Society at the same time. Late afternoon on a weekday would do. The girls would then come with the adult women needed to provide proper chaperonage before, during, and after the activities judged by the local members (and not the missionaries) to be a proper way to develop the youth. Our desire to make a statement of strict adherence to morality would have been preserved because we would have conveyed the truth of our message in the behavior pattern of their own Guatemalan understanding.

Behavior says things. Because behavior says things, I believe that we, as Mormons, must abandon the adherence to precise patterned behavior as a definition of Mormonness. We all sing the hymn "Do What Is Right." I have no problem with that when it means keep the commandments. Honoring parents, respecting God, not killing or committing adultery, and refraining from stealing are understood and understandable in all cultures. We must, however, give up the attempt to "do what is right" in the sense of performing Church obligations and programs in a particular way around the whole earth. Procedural uniformity may make members comfortable when they travel about the Church, but it tends to make many local Saints uncomfortable, it unnecessarily harms them when they are forced into isolation from their non-Mormon friends and kin, and it blocks the fullest understanding needed for missionary work. Rather, if we are to become a world church, we must march to a different tune. The hymn which I believe captures the task of the world church is "Oh Say, What Is Truth?" though not as the question posed by the hymn, but rather as a declaration of what we must do: say what is truth in the distinctive behavior and distinctive language of every region. If we always attempt to say what is truth, in whatever appropriate behavioral form that truth is best transmitted, then we will always be able to communicate with the nonmembers in the surrounding cultural system. They will always understand what we intended them to understand because we say the truth in the idiom of their behavior system "according to the language of their own understanding." If we try to standardize the behavior of Mormons and Mormon religious practice worldwide, we will always be forcing Mormons outside the western United States to be misunderstood by their compatriots, since the local meaning of the standardized performances will vary from place to place, even within the United States. The misunderstanding inevitably isolates the Mormons. We want Mormons to be a peculiar people, but we want them to be peculiar because their behavior truthfully conveys their principles.

Only when we abandon the proposition of procedural "do what is right" and begin to flexibly "say what is truth," will we move from a Utah-American church, with a scattering of isolated Americanized enclaves, to a world church. To make this transition we must abandon the attempt to define the proper form of Mormon behavior. That needs to be done uniquely for each culture, not once for the world. We must give the people of each culture the flexibility and the right to say what is truth according to the behavioral possibilities of their own behavioral dictionaries. Accordingly, there must be enormous trust in the regional leaders, who must be raised in the local culture. Those who travel to supervise the task must be flexible enough to hear the gospel message on drums in those areas where drums are "good," on guitars where guitars are "good," and on pianos and organs where drums and guitars are "bad." Not only will we get the message across better and faster and more acceptably, but we will save the not inconsiderable cost of shipping pianos to Guatemala and Zaire, where pianos are neither playable nor "good."

The moment we move in this direction, we see that the gospel is not a set of behavioral procedures to be followed to the letter. That is the Pharisaical tradition which Christ rebuked. Rather, the gospel is a set of principles, among them faith, morality, and responsibility to others through covenants. These principles are not present in all cultures, though I do believe that each of the world's cultures already understands some of the gospel principles very well, if not better than we do. (Genealogical concern for ancestors is an obvious example.) Our task is to take the principles to the various societies of the earth and let the people speak the principles in their behavior according to the meanings of behavior in that region. "Teach them correct principles and let them govern themselves" becomes the watchword of variety and openness in the emerging world church.

We are not divided by differences of behavior, any more than we are divided by differences of language. What is important and what unites us is the common adherence to the central principles, the core premises of morality and a covenanted responsibility to each other — the culture of the gospel. We must learn to ignore "do what is right" in the formalist sense and exert ourselves to "say what is truth" and glory in the knowledge that the proper way to say the truth will entail different behavior from region to region on this earth. Thus, we must become accepting and tolerant of behavioral difference among the brothers and sisters who would speak the truth in their different actions in every corner of the world.

Too often we see the cultural and performative differences among Mormons around the world as a manifestation of disunity that differing cultures impose on the gospel. For us, gospel unity implies all of us doing the same things in similar ways, often in imported cinderblock chapels. I believe the notion is wrong. If we are united, it will be because we are proclaiming the same message to our non-Mormon brothers and sisters. But if we are to tell them the message, it must be in their own language of verbal and behavioral meanings. That means that we who would be united can be united only if we are sending and receiving the same message. And to send the same message we must be both speaking and behaving differently in each culture area of the earth. Differences do not divide us. Gospel unity will come from the differences, by virtue of proclaiming the shared message through the diverse languages of our behavior. If we do not allow great behavioral flexibility, we will have accomplished the analog of having taught English to every foreigner who wants to believe the truths of the gospel, at which point they will be so isolated from their non-Mormon compatriots that they will be unable to share the gospel with them. Indeed, if we attempt to gain substantial behavioral similarity among Mormons of different cultural regions, the similarities of behavior will divide us, for, like it or not, the similarities of behavior will be conveying messages different from the message originally intended.

We must seek unity in the expression of truth by encouraging appropriate divergence of behavior, according to the differences in the meaning of particular behaviors in each region of the earth. That is the complicated task that looms before us in the next decades, as we attempt to be a world church. We must learn to grow comfortable with — and trusting of — local procedures that must be different from our own if we are to make the gospel intelligible to people of different behavioral systems. I believe that the perspective "say what is truth" according to the behavior and language of one's own understanding will facilitate an easier transition to a world church than "do as I'm doing; follow, follow me" and, in the end, I think we will be gratified by having kept the differences.

INDIVIDUALITY AND COMMUNITY

As we learn in studying about the Savior, the example of a single life well lived can be far more motivating, and ultimately rewarding, than all the easy accolades of our peers.

— KAREN LYNN DAVIDSON

Peer Pressure and the Truly Adult Woman

KAREN LYNN DAVIDSON

*S*ooner or later, in almost any discussion of social problems, someone will pin the blame for those problems on a villain familiar to all of us. That villain is *peer pressure*. Everyone nods knowingly. Oh yes, peer pressure!

We seem to be sure of two things about peer pressure. First, we know it's usually negative. Peer pressure means pressure to misbehave, try drugs, drive too fast, ignore the advice of parents. And second, we know it's mainly a problem for our young people, something we worry about for our children, not for ourselves. The day our second-grader comes home from school with that first filthy word, so carefully taught her by one of her advanced classmates, we want to sweep her up in our arms and run as fast as we can to an isolated cabin somewhere on a beautiful mountaintop, where we can make sure that everything she sees and hears is uplifting, wholesome, and beneficial. We feel angry with whoever taught her that bad word. How different life would be for that child if it weren't for those friends! We're forced to teach "just say no" as a rather wide-sweeping response, not just because her friends might suggest drugs some day, but because they might suggest all kinds of destructive, unacceptable things. We're almost convinced that for children, friends are a liability. Where is that insurance policy we can sign up for to make sure that each of our children goes through life with a group of wise, under-

Karen Lynn Davidson, who holds a Ph.D. in English literature from the University of Southern California, was a member of the Brigham Young University English faculty for ten years and also served as director of the BYU Honors Program. Her Church callings have included stake Relief Society education counselor and membership on the Relief Society Writing Committee, Church Music Committee, and Hymnbook Executive Committee.

standing, mature, stable, delightful, studious, law-abiding, sensitive friends?

But peer pressure is not a problem limited to young people. It is also part of our adult world. It's true that we're influenced by the scriptures, we're influenced by the counsel of our Church leaders, we're influenced by those responses that come to us after we've uttered a heartfelt prayer. But we adults are also influenced by our friends.

I believe the question of peer pressure in our lives deserves some thought. What control does peer pressure have over us? Could we be more selective about the way we respond to peer pressure and put it to better use in our lives? If you're like me, peer pressure can work two ways. In one instance it may keep us from doing what we should, but another time it may be exactly what we need to keep us on our toes. When our Father in Heaven answers our prayers or chooses to send a message to us, is it possible that He sometimes does so through the medium of peer pressure?

When I was a little girl I had some nursery rhyme phonograph records, and one of my favorite songs went like this:

> There was a jolly miller once,
>   Lived on the river Dee;
> He worked and sang from morn till night,
>   No lark more blithe than he.
> And this the burden of his song
>   Forever used to be,
> I care for everyone, everywhere
>   And everyone cares for me.

Many years later, as a college student, I spotted this nursery rhyme in *The Annotated Mother Goose*. Much to my surprise, the original verse was quite different from the one I knew. This poem about the happy miller and the reason he was so full of joy had been censored on my phonograph record. The last four lines actually go like this:

> And this the burden of his song
>   Forever used to be,

> I care for nobody, no! not I,
> If nobody cares for me.

(William S. Baring-Gould and Cecil Baring-Gould, *The Annotated Mother Goose* [New York: Bramhall House, 1962], p. 103.)

Which version of this nursery rhyme is more true to life — the positive version that says the miller is happy because he shares love with all around him, or the cynical version that says he is happy because he keeps to himself? Which is the key to happiness — involvement or isolation? Most of us would vote for involvement. For one thing, in the Latter-day Saint church we don't have a hermit tradition in any form. A life lived in seclusion just isn't our version of a holy life, though for some others it is. And besides, the miller apparently had a choice that just isn't open to most of us. Family and other responsibilities mean that we are interacting with others constantly. We observe them, and we measure our actions, our appearance, even our spirituality by what we observe. They give us messages, spoken and unspoken, about their measurement of us, and their opinions do count for us.

So peer pressure is there; we can't ignore it. Furthermore, to be completely out of touch with the day-to-day influences of other people is not a sign of good emotional health. But a preoccupation with the good opinion of society brings with it a serious disadvantage: it becomes a sufficient goal in and of itself. Perhaps, more than the dangers of peer pressure, it is the dangers of peer acceptance that we should be concerned with.

Each morning, to start the day, a small percentage of the members of our Church read a chapter from the scriptures or some other high-minded message to set the tone for the day and guide their aspirations, while a huge percentage of members of the Church read "Dear Abby"; she's there with advice every day, too. If you gauge your life according to her advice, you can't go too far wrong in public opinion. Abigail van Buren is a woman of great common sense and even compassion. But is her advice column a source of celestial counsel? According to her, the right to privacy can supersede another person's need for kindness; the value of peace in the family can be more important than making known one's views regarding standards of personal morality. In some cases, she may be right. But "Dear Abby" is the voice of today's standards, not the voice of eternal truth. These are two different measures of behavior.

It is admirable to stay out of jail, carry out one's duties, avoid social criticism, and live life as a responsible citizen. If we do these things, peer acceptance is ours. Other people don't scold us, punish us, or look down on us. We fit right in. But the danger of measuring our lives and characters only by Abby's standard is that we may come to think this standard, the standard of peer acceptance, is sufficient; we may never sense the potential that resides in our spiritual natures.

Many of you have read a story by Leo Tolstoy called "The Death of Ivan Ilyich." If you have not, put it next on your list. If you read it carefully, it will hit, almost with the impact of scripture. It tells the story of Ivan Ilyich, a well-to-do government official in Russia. One day he injures himself, and although this bruise does not at first seem to be serious, Ivan becomes more and more ill. Finally, it is clear that the doctors have done all they can. Ivan Ilyich lies on his deathbed, and he has plenty of time to think about how he has lived. "Dear Abby," had she known him, would have seen little in his life to criticize. But Ivan, now trapped in pain and panic from which he sees no release, begins to realize that he has been satisfied with a standard that was not a saintly one. " 'Maybe I did not live as I ought to have done,' it suddenly occurred to him. 'But how could that be, when I did everything properly?' " (Leo Tolstoy, *The Death of Ivan Ilyich and Other Stories* [New York: New American Library, 1960], p. 148.)

This is Tolstoy's message: "Doing everything properly" falls remarkably short of the standard set by Jesus Christ. Peer acceptance, which is often not based on His standards, gives us a false sense of adequacy and achievement. As adults, not many of us have someone pulling at our sleeve coaxing, "Don't be out of it. Try marijuana just this once." It is not peer pressure in this sense that we need to fear. It is social *acceptance* that we need to be careful of. If we seek nothing higher, it can paralyze our aspirations. We have weighed ourselves in the balance of common-sense civic virtue and found ourselves not wanting at all. For every fault we may see in ourselves, we can quickly think of someone far worse, and a few cliches about "being only human" exonerate us from a whole list of offenses; we wouldn't want to aim too high or be too hard on ourselves, after all!

But suppose we draw most of our friends and social activities from among other Latter-day Saints. Doesn't social acceptance take on a different meaning then? If we are active Church members, welcome in our wards and interacting every day among other Church members, couldn't we say that peer acceptance represents a high standard? Yes, I think there would be some truth in this. But a plateau is a plateau. The very things that are the badges of peer acceptance in the local ward — adherence to the Word of Wisdom, payment of tithing, fulfillment of a Church calling, attendance at Church meetings — may begin to seem sufficient in themselves. President Harold B. Lee said, "This gospel is not a gospel of being. It is a gospel of becoming." In spite of those smiles of appreciation from other ward members when we walk into the chapel, in spite of the satisfaction of being seen as a model member, just "being" is not enough. The sudden withdrawal of peer acceptance may let us know when we have transgressed, but winning peer acceptance guarantees only a minimum standard. It is not an assurance that we are moving every day toward the pattern of a divine example.

The friends who know us best may be the most inclined to tolerate our shortcomings rather than help us note them. They may tiptoe around our bad temper so that *they* are the ones who become skillful in handling the problem of *our* temper; we aren't required to mend our ways at all. They may indulgently redefine our stubbornness as strength of character. They may redefine our cynicism as shrewd common sense, our lack of commitment as serene detachment, our vanity as self-respect.

177

When we are preoccupied with peer acceptance, our energies are fragmented in some ways that really drain us. We must be continually comparing ourselves with trends and norms. In my ward in Southern California, beautiful long fingernails have become so common that they are almost taken for granted as part of good grooming. They may be acrylic fingernails, or they may be long and highly polished fingernails of one's own. Both my visiting teachers have beautiful fingernails; so do all three of the sisters whom I visit. Should I be saying to myself, "Karen, where is your self-respect? What kind of fingernails are those?" I have to stop for a moment and remind myself what a superficial concern this is. I have to say to myself, consciously, "That isn't for you; they don't mix with music or with typing; for someone else they're important, but for you they aren't. Surely, when you attend Relief Society, you can think about something better than fingernail tallies: 'Let's see, out of nine of us sitting on this row, there are six sets of beautiful nails, one set polished but not long, one other set that looks like mine. . . .' "

It is wonderful when we can just step forth as our own selves, confident that most right-thinking people will be happy to accept us on our own terms, not with the feeling we have to pass an audition or be checked off according to some rating form. Then we can save our energies for more important concerns. If we are trying every minute to meet the expectations of some person or group, this exacts a high toll from our nerves and our energies. In "The Love Song of J. Alfred Prufrock," T. S. Eliot created a character who has been described as merely a name with a voice. Prufrock has no identity, no sense of self, no feeling of purpose. And two of the most devastating lines Prufrock speaks in the whole poem are these:

> There will be time, there will be time
> To prepare a face to meet the faces that you meet. . . .

(T. S. Eliot, "The Love Song of J. Alfred Prufrock," in *Collected Poems, 1909-1962* [New York: Harcourt, Brace and World, 1963], lines 26–27.)

What kind of a life is this, to feel that we must put on a new face, like a mask, in order to try to please each person? For one thing, it's an exhausting life. The strain of this effort deflects our attentions and energies from the task of just going ahead and "becoming."

If we routinely accept the social norms that surround us, we may become deaf to a voice inside that wishes us to act in a different way. Several years ago, William Dyer, a faculty member of the BYU School of Management, gave a forum address titled "On Becoming an Authentic, Congruent Person." I have never forgotten that talk. An authentic, congruent person is the opposite of J. Alfred Prufrock. An authentic, congruent person never has to prepare a new face for a new situation. I was particularly impressed with this anecdote that Professor Dyer related:

"Some years ago I decided to try to respond more directly to my own warm and loving feelings when it was appropriate according to my values. I had noticed with my four sons that when they were young, I would hug and kiss them. But as they grew older for some reason I stopped that most satisfying behavior. I discovered that I still felt like showing my affection and reasoned that to be more congruent I should act more directly. I decided to hug and kiss my sons, and to share openly this affection, particularly when I would leave or return from a trip. I've always been able to share affection with my daughter, but with my sons, as the scripture says, there was the 'fear of men.' I think my boys were a little uneasy at first at this revival of physical affection. But I also think that they liked this response from their father.

"One day I was faced with an interesting situation. One of my sons offered to take me to the airport as I was leaving on a trip. He invited a young lady to drive with us. When we got to the airport I thought, 'Should I hug and kiss my son as I usually do, or would that embarrass him with this young lady present?' I then concluded that I had the right feelings. He also knew that I was a kissing father, and that was *his* problem. If he didn't like that, then he would have to be congruent and let me know. So I hugged and kissed my son as usual. There was no apparent embarrassment in him, and I think he would have been disappointed in me had I abandoned our usual practice. At that point, *not* doing that would have been an incongruent act on my part."

Authenticity and individuality are wonderful qualities, and we must not let a false feeling of accountability to society sap the vigor from these traits. Nevertheless, we are social beings; we live in groups. As Latter-day Saints, we choose to meet together partly because we think we have something to derive from one another—something more important than seeing if we are the last holdout with short fingernails.

As Latter-day Saints, we agree on the great persuading force of example. The ultimate example for our earthly lives is our Savior, Jesus Christ. We can study His life; we can live so that we feel His presence, so that His spirit will influence our attitudes and our decisions. We tell our teenagers, "Conduct yourselves so that if the Savior were with you in your car tonight, you would be proud to have Him as a witness of everything you do and say."

But that's an abstraction. In a literal sense, the Savior is not physically present in that car or in our home. What does He do when He needs to give us a very direct message? I feel that what He often does is to delegate one of His sons and daughters to be the conduit of His message. We know He sends many kinds of blessings to His children through others of His children. Why would He not bless us by raising up an example for us when we need it? He may not speak to us in person; He may not even send us a telegram; but what He very well may do is send one of His other children to represent an example we need to see.

In pondering the question of peer pressure, the important distinction we must make is this: although the acceptance of our peers may represent nothing more than an agreed-upon standard of minimum decency, the individual example of one of our friends or family members can represent a Christlike standard. When we need to have a particular weakness made known to us, a neighbor, a member of our ward, a visiting teacher may appear right in front of us, usually without being aware of the mission she is fulfilling, to act out the strength we must cultivate.

But it's easier to talk about responding to these examples and learning from them than it is to actually respond. Let me tell you one problem I have. I live in a wonderful ward, and I need do nothing more than look around my Relief Society to see fine examples of godly women. But when I begin taking note of these examples, what is my first reaction? I feel crummy. I feel inferior and discouraged. I can go down my entire Relief Society roster and be intimidated by every name on the list. Why can't I cook like Sally Cauch? Why can't I have an organized household like Anne McCullough? Why can't I sing like Christie Frandsen? Why can't I be as fit as Teresa Rinallo?

I think the trouble is that my approach is artificial. I'm doing exactly what we've been saying not to: I'm keeping score; I'm measuring. I'm tending to see others at their best and myself at my worst. When another person's example has influenced my life, I haven't come across that example by going down the Relief Society roster or by checking out so many sets of fingernails. The examples seem to have arisen naturally. They have been there when I've needed them, *because* I've needed them.

When I became a stepmother, one little stepson was nine and the other was four. I was overwhelmed not by the joy of my new role but by its seriousness. I was determined to be reasonable, fair, consistent, and responsible. So I often heard myself saying things like, "Eliott, that toast is not burned; it's your toast, and you will eat it right now. You don't need to be so silly." I had to watch my mother and my sister, both of whom were experienced mothers, indulge my stepsons before I realized that at least sometimes I could just say, "All right. We'll fix another toast for you if you don't want that one." They were much more at ease, much more accepting. I had been inclined to say, "If you can't find your tennis shoes, then you haven't looked very hard. You look until you find them, and I mean right now. They are *your* shoes, and you had better have them on *your* feet by the time we leave in three minutes." They showed me that I was just as far ahead to respond to this little crisis by saying, "Well then, let's hunt! I'm sure your shoes are around here someplace. Now where could they have gone?"

My change was quite sudden. As soon as I saw how differently my mother and sister treated my stepsons, it struck me how out of line I had been. I became more patient, less rule-oriented; I just needed to see an example of that kind of behavior. But I hate to think how long it might have taken me to mend my ways if the example of my mother and my sister had not been there for me to see. As reluctant as I am to admit this, I have to say that even if I had had a front row seat at general conference and heard one of the Brethren address the Church on the subject of patience, I'm afraid it still would have washed right over me. I wouldn't have related his talk to my problem. I needed something more direct. I could have heard — in fact, taught — a Relief Society lesson on patience and gone home and still acted the role of the critical, rigid, unbending enforcer. It was example that caught my attention and compelled me to change this wrong, pointless pattern that was making everyone so unhappy. I could ease up; I could let things go. Examples give us inspiration. In this case, the example also gave me permission.

I am greatly indebted to my friends and relatives for many other examples that have been crucial to my life. I didn't marry until I was thirty-eight years old; the fact that I was able to establish a productive and very happy life as a single woman is something I owe largely to the happy single women who are my friends. No book could have taught me that. I had to see them doing it. I feel privileged to be partly responsible for a new hymn in our hymnbook—number 197, "Each Life That Touches Ours for Good"—that gives us the opportunity to praise our Heavenly Father for the blessing of fine friends.

Most of us sometime in our Church experience have heard someone say, "The Lord doesn't really *punish* us by sending us to a lower kingdom. He just knows where we'll be the most comfortable." I don't know if this is true doctrine or not, but I think the notion is true. All of us have righteous, Christlike friends in whose presence we want to feel comfortable. The minute we feel out of tune, ill at ease in the presence of such a friend, that feeling is a useful warning. The Lord has placed many righteous people on this earth. If we are seeking to perfect ourselves, we will desire the company of these people. We will feel comfortable with them.

As a teacher of literature, I agree with the observation that in literature, evil is often more interesting than good. There is no such thing as a fascinating novel populated entirely by saintly people. But in real life, I believe the reverse is true. Good is more interesting than evil. I think the Lord will cause us to be drawn toward the good. We will find it more interesting. Suppose the house on either side of yours is sold, and into each house moves a new family. One of the families is a decent, average family. They watch a great deal of television, they get most excited when they talk about the new motorboat they are planning to buy—they are an ordinary family, with an ordinary vision of themselves. The other family, by contrast, seeks virtue. They devote their summers to assisting in a camp for asthmatic children, they instill nonmaterialistic values in their children, they strive for saintly goals that have nothing to do with what television tells them is important in life. Which family is more interesting? Which one arrests your attention?

I assure you that all around us are messages in the form of example that our Father in Heaven wishes us to heed. The goodness, the productive creativity, and the righteous energies that we can see in our family and associates are immense. The Lord inspires different ones of His children to great spiritual heights in different ways.

We do not all need to be the same. Sameness is one of the false premises of peer pressure. One of the most important things we come to learn as adult women is that two profoundly different people may both be fine, devoted members of the Church. But we can never and in many instances should never want to escape the influence or expectations of our peers. Among them we must recognize the example of those whose lives have reached a higher plane than that required for mere group acceptance. I feel that sometimes, when the Lord wishes to show us with great impact a better way to be and live, He uses concrete examples of such lives — our friends — to teach us what to do. As we learn in studying about the Savior, the example of a single life well lived can be far more motivating, and ultimately rewarding, than all the easy accolades of our peers. To be attentive to the virtues of others can open wonderful new doors. To settle into nothing higher than comfortable social acceptability is a mistake. The responsibility is ours to know the difference.

Thoughts of a Grasshopper

Louise Plummer

I first became acquainted with the story of the grass-hopper and the ant as a young girl—not by reading Aesop's fable, but by seeing a Walt Disney cartoon. In the cartoon the grasshopper fiddles and sings and eats the leaves off trees while the ants are gathering food to store for the winter. The queen of ants warns him that he'd better prepare for winter too, but the grasshopper continues fiddling and singing. When winter comes, the grasshopper, blue from cold, can no longer play his fiddle. In desperation, he knocks on the tree where the ants live and begs them to let him in. The queen of ants gives her "I-told-you-so" speech and ends with, "So take your fiddle and"—there is a long pause—"and play." So the grasshopper earns the warmth and food of the ants by playing his fiddle.

Aesop, in contrast, is not as kind to the grasshopper. When he comes begging for food, the ant merely tells him, "You sang through the summer; now you can dance through the winter."

I remind you of this story so that I can tell you that even as a child, it made me uncomfortable. It still makes me un-comfortable. The story of the grasshopper and the ant makes me uncomfortable because *I am a grasshopper.* I dance in elevators. The second the door closes, I begin tap dancing and flinging my arms wildly about. I make faces and stick my tongue out at the hidden cameras I believe exist in every elevator. When the doors open, I stop short and stare with what I hope is a bored elevator look into the open hallway ahead.

Louise Plummer is a wife and the mother of four boys. She has a master's degree in English from the University of Minnesota and is the author of a young adult novel, The Romantic Obsessions and Humiliations of Annie Sehlmeier *(Delacorte Press). She teaches writing at Brigham Young University and has served as a Primary teacher in the Oak Hills Fifth Ward in Provo, Utah.*

185

I am a grasshopper. It takes me a full day to dismantle my Christmas tree because I dress up in the decorations. I wrap the gold tinsel around my head like a turban. I make a shawl for my neck from glass beads and paper chains. I have a special pair of vampy red high heels that I wear only on the day I undecorate the tree. Red glass balls hang from my ears. I sing in front of the hall mirror. I sing "New York, New York—if you can make it there, you'll make it anywhere." I don't know who wrote it, but it's the kind of song that can make you a star.

I am a grasshopper. I have never prepared for winter or the Apocalypse. I do have two thousand pounds of wheat that I hope never to eat and a box of chocolate chips that won't last through next week. Last summer I tried to bottle some peaches—the cold pack method—just to see if I could do it. I bottled three jars full. They sit in my freezer like museum pieces.

I am a grasshopper. I live in a metaphorical world. I read and write fiction. I draw pictures. I dance in elevators. I sing dressed in Christmas tree decorations.

But I was raised by ants. My mother and father emigrated from the Netherlands to America in 1948 with four children. Five more children were born in Salt Lake City. My father was an electrician. My mother kept the house and us immaculately. She knitted us sweaters and baked our bread. Dinner was ready each night at 5:30 on the nose. She taught me the correct principles of work. She forced me to wash woodwork, wax floors, and clean behind the toilet, but my priorities were not the same as hers. My distress is recorded in my journal of 1959 when I was sixteen years old. The first entry reads:

"Mother has just blown her top. I am a lazy bum with no sense of responsibility, and all I do is write stories and draw and visit my friends. According to her I am no good. Which is not altogether true, but not altogether false either. I already knew everything she told me, so she really didn't have to get all fired up."

Another entry:

"I hate to get up in the morning. This morning, Mother started yelling for me to get up at the unearthly hour of 11:00. Then every five minutes, she'd come in and say, 'Are you getting up now or not?' Then I would say, 'Do I have a choice?' As soon as she leaves the room I lie back down and daydream. I like to stay in bed so that I can daydream."

And finally: "Mother is mad because she can't find the little top thing to the pressure cooker and since I was the last one to use the pressure cooker, I lost it. Well, I didn't!"

Even from these excerpts you can tell that I considered my work to be different from my mother's. I was already writing, drawing, and daydreaming. And I never outgrew it. I never intended to. If growing up meant leaving behind the imagination I loved, I didn't want to be grown up, at least, not in the same way as most of the adults I knew.

As much as I love my mother, I have not grown up in her image. But I admire her work. I love to open her linen closet and see the neatly folded sheets and pillow cases, color-coordinated, meticulously stacked. I like to stand in front of the year's supply in her dust-free basement and admire the rows of preserves, of laundry soap, of peanut butter, and of polyunsaturated oils. I like to see her white — really white — laundry blowing on the clothesline. I like to ask her for the kinds of things that I can never find in my own house, like the negative of a picture taken twenty years ago or a darning needle. She always knows where such things are located.

I clean too. I'm not always on top of it like my mother, but I do something my mother doesn't do — I write lists of things I clean up. Here's a list from my journal, dated March 3, 1984, Saturday:

"What we found when we cleaned under our bed:

"Books: one triple combination; *A Mormon Mother*, by Annie Tanner; *The Clown*, by Heinrich Böll; *The Tin Drum*, by Günter Grass; *An Essay on Criticism*, by Graham Hough; *The Labyrinthe of Solitude*, by Octavio Paz; the December '83 *National Geographic*; the Roseville phone directory; *Be My Guest*, by Conrad Hilton; the April '83 *Popular Photography; Time* magazine, February 27, 1984; Louise's journal — March 1977;

The Power of Positive Thinking, by Norman Vincent Peale; one
Reader's Digest (February '84) including the titles 'My Angry
Son' and 'Advice from Sexually Happy Wives'
    "One set of Tom's office keys
    "A photograph of Sam and Louise
    "Photograph of Tom and completed jigsaw puzzle
    "A letter from Roseville schools about Jonathan's registra-
tion
    "Dishes: one red mixing bowl; two saucers; two mugs; one
kitchen knife; one empty cherry cola can; one empty Häagen-
Daz chocolate chip carton with lid; one melmac cup
    "One rotex labeler
    "One broken toothbrush holder
    "One photograph of Dave and Sue Salmon and girls
    "One empty raisin carton
    "Four black lead pencils
    "One red lead pencil
    "Five felt tip pens
    "One ball point pen
    "One roll of packing tape
    "One cloth handkerchief
    "One pair of pantyhose
    "One black high heel shoe
    "Two plastic clown heads
    "One plastic race car
    "One page from the church directory
    "Two pen caps
    "One broken dart
    "One hanger
    "One bank deposit slip
    "One seminary work sheet (Exodus 24, 25, and 27)
    "One white shoe lace
    "One yellow wrapping ribbon
    "One Roseville bank envelope
    "One disposable razor
    "Three yellow legal pads, one is filled with notes on how
to get rich, including the title 'You Can Negotiate Anything'
    "One stake directory

"One plastic action figure

"One pair of scissors

"One metal whistle

"One roll of toilet paper

"Notes by Tom on developing a seasonal recreational facility for ultralites, golf, fishing, horseback riding, cross-country skiing, and key words from Norman Vincent Peale: *visualize, prayerize, actualize*

"One empty Kleenex box

"One score sheet from Yahtzee

"One belt

"One piece of chalk

"One orange peel AND

"One popsicle stick."

I'm not completely comfortable with this list, just as I haven't always been comfortable with being a grasshopper. I always wondered if there was a room in a family of ants for a grasshopper, room in a community of ants for a grasshopper, or room in a church of ants for a grasshopper. My discomfort, I believe, comes from my fear of disapproval, my fear that ants will not accept me unless I am just like them.

I take comfort in Flannery O'Connor's short story, "Revelation," in which Mrs. Turpin, a middle-aged Christian Southern woman, views mankind as a hierarchy: "On the bottom of the heap were most colored people; . . . then next to them — not above, just away from — were the white trash; then above them were the home-owners, and above them the home-and-land owners, to which she and Claud belonged. Above she [sic] and Claud were people with a lot of money and much bigger houses and much more land." (Flannery O'Connor, "Revelation," in *Everything That Rises Must Converge* [New York: Farrar, Straus and Giroux, 1965], p. 217.)

At the end of the story, Mrs. Turpin receives a vision that destroys her delusion of a hierarchy. She sees a " vast swinging bridge extending upward from the earth through a field of living fire. Upon it a vast horde of souls were rumbling toward heaven. There were whole companies of white trash, clean for the first time in their lives, and bands of black niggers in white robes, and battalions of freaks and lunatics shouting and clapping and leaping like frogs. And bringing up the end of the procession was a tribe of people . . . marching behind the others with great dignity, accountable as they had always been for good order and common sense and respectable behavior. They alone were on key. Yet she could see by their shocked and altered faces that even their virtues were being burned away." (O'Connor, p. 238.)

I like this story because it is about redemption. Without the atonement of Jesus Christ, our virtues, whatever they are, are meaningless. We are all equally human.

King Benjamin asks, "Are we all not beggars?" (Mosiah 4:19.)

"What about works?" someone may ask. "Don't ants work harder than grasshoppers?"

No. Grasshoppers work differently from ants.

I would like to rewrite the ending of "The Grasshopper and the Ants" like this: It is winter, and the grasshopper is walking in the snow, talking to herself and answering herself. She wears a yellow slicker over her sweater because she can't find her parka (which is buried in the debris under her bed). Because she was out of groceries this morning, she is eating a brownie with a carton of milk bought at the 7-Eleven which, thank heaven, is open 365 days a year. The door in the tree where the ants live swings open. The queen ant appears and says to the grasshopper, "We are bored to death. Won't you tell us a story or at least a good joke? Our teenagers are driving us crazy; maybe you could write them a play to perform, or just a roadshow? Do you have any ideas for a daddy-daughter party?"

The grasshopper replies that she has ideas for all of them. So the ant invites her in and seats her at a spotless kitchen table with pencil and paper, and the grasshopper writes the roadshow.

The ant feeds her guest a slice of homemade bread, fresh from the oven, and a glass of freshly squeezed orange juice. "How do you get all of these ideas?" she asks the grasshopper.

190

"They come to me," says the grasshopper, "while I am taking long hot baths."

I am a grasshopper. I work hard at writing, at teaching, at singing and dancing, at mothering. I have taught my four boys some grasshopper ways. They all can make chocolate chip cookies and brownies without a recipe.

My mother used to say, "I don't know where you came from." This bothered me, because if she didn't know, I certainly didn't. But I found out where I came from years later when I went back to Holland for the first time since I was five years old. I stayed with my paternal grandmother — Oma — who lived in Utrecht. She set her alarm for nine o'clock in the morning. When I saw that, I knew where I came from. I came from Oma.

I came from you, too, Mother. Otherwise, I would never clean under my bed.

I came from God.